Luftwaffe
Sturmgruppen

M000304840

OSPREY
PUBLISHING

Luftwaffe
Sturmgruppen

John Weal

Series editor Tony Holmes

Front Cover

By Christmas Eve 1944, Hitler's ill-fated counter-offensive through the Ardennes – the 'Battle of the Bulge', launched just eight days earlier – was already in trouble. The bad weather which the Führer had counted upon to protect his forces from Allied air attack had failed to last. The early morning mists of 23 December had slowly lifted to reveal a clear, steely-blue winter sky. The following day the Eighth Air Force was up in strength, with no fewer than 2046 B-17 and B-24 'heavies' being despatched against Luftwaffe airfields and transportation targets behind the battle front.

Warned of the enemy's approach, IV./JG 3 scrambled 30 Fw 190s from its Gütersloh base at 1130 hrs. After an hour in the air, they were vectored onto a large formation of Flying Fortresses nearing the German frontier south of Aachen. Contact was made over Liège, in Belgium – one of the very few occasions that the *Gruppe* engaged the enemy outside the borders of the Reich. *Gruppenkommandeur* Hauptmann Hubert-York Weydenhammer led his pilots in a wide climbing turn to port to get behind the US bombers before giving the order to attack.

Flying 'Yellow 19', Fahnenjunker-Feldwebel Wilhelm Hopfensitz, whose first victory had been one of the 30 B-26 Marauders claimed by IV./JG 3 the day before, was determined to add a four-engined 'heavy' to his score. Selecting one of the outer Flying Fortresses on the starboard side of the 487th Bomb Group's middle squadron, Hopfensitz bored in close. When the B-17 was filling his sights, he let fly with his 30 mm cannon. The bomber staggered under the impact of the large calibre cannon shells and slowly went down.

Encouraged by this success, Hopfensitz broke away before coming back in to line up on a second victim. But so intent was he on getting his approach just right that he completely failed to notice that he was also overhauling a B-17 of the 487th's low squadron flying little more than 100 ft (30 m) below him. One of the gunners from this unknown aircraft put a burst of fire into the engine of Hopfensitz's Focke-Wulf.

Abandoning all thoughts of a second kill, the young pilot took to his parachute and ended up in Allied captivity. Post-war records would indicate that his first victim, the 838th Bomb Squadron's B-17G 43-37979, also survived long enough to be written-off in a forced-landing at Le Culot airfield southeast of Brussels (*Cover artwork by Mark Postlethwaite*)

First published in Great Britain in 2005 by Osprey Publishing
Midland House, West Way, Botley, Oxford, OX2 0PH
E-mail: info@ospreypublishing.com

ISBN 1 84176 908 8

Edited by Tony Holmes
Page layouts by Mark Holt
Cover Artwork by Mark Postlethwaite
Aircraft Profiles by John Weal
Originated by PPS-Grasmere Ltd, Leeds, UK
Printed in China through Bookbuilders

05 06 07 08 09   10 9 8 7 6 5 4 3 2 1

Buy online at www.ospreypublishing.com

ACKNOWLEDGEMENTS
The author would like to thank the following individuals for their generous help in providing information and photographs:
Karl-Heinz Berger, Oskar Bösch, Eddie J Creek, Roger Freeman, Chris Goss, Manfred Griehl, Rolf Hase, Gerhard Kott, Walter Matthiesen, Eric Mombeek, Axel Paul, Tomás Poruba, Dr Alfred Price, Ernst Schröder, Jerry Scutts, Robert Simpson and Ulrich Weber.

EDITOR'S NOTE
To make this series as authoritative as possible, the Editor would be interested in hearing from any individual who may have relevant photographs, documentation or first-hand experiences relating to the world's elite units, their pilots and their aircraft, of the various theatres of war. Any material used will be credited to its original source. Please contact Tony Holmes via e-mail at: tony.holmes@osprey-jets.freeserve.co.uk

CONTENTS

STURMSTAFFEL 1 – TRIAL BY FIRE

'I have volunteered for the *Sturmstaffel* of my own free will. I fully understand the fundamental principles of the *Staffel*.

1. All attacks will, without exception, be carried out in formation and to within the closest possible range of the enemy.
2. Losses suffered during the approach will be compensated for by immediately closing up on the formation leader.
3. The enemy under attack is to be shot down from the shortest range possible or, if this is unsuccessful, destroyed by ramming.
4. The *Sturm* pilot will remain in contact with the stricken enemy until the point of impact with the ground has been established.

'I voluntarily accept the obligation to abide by these principles, and will not return to base without having destroyed my enemy. Should I violate these principles, I am prepared to face court martial or dismissal from the *Staffel*.'

When the first dozen or so volunteer pilots put their signatures to this extraordinary document on 17 November 1943, they were opening a new chapter in the long-running story of the daylight defence of Hitler's Reich.

That story had begun more than four years earlier with the first tentative attacks across the North Sea by machines of RAF Bomber Command. These initial incursions had been given short shrift by the Luftwaffe's fighter defences. Of the 34 Wellingtons despatched against naval targets on the two raids of 14 and 18 December 1939, exactly half had been shot down – and this without their even penetrating the German mainland (see *Osprey Aircraft of the Aces 11 – Bf 109D/E Aces 1939–41* for further details)! Little wonder, therefore, that the British quickly reconsidered their strategic policy and henceforth restricted the RAF's bombing campaign against Germany primarily to the hours of darkness.

It was America's entry into the war two years later which rekindled the spark of daylight bombing. Confident in the power of their four-engined B-17 Flying Fortresses and B-24 Liberators, and of their reputed ability to 'place a bomb in a pickle barrel', the USAAF was wholly committed to daylight precision bombing. The Americans resisted all attempts to persuade them to add their numbers to the loose streams of RAF bombers now raiding Germany almost nightly. They would instead adhere rigidly to their tight daylight formations.

In time, these two diametrically opposed national policies would combine to form the 'round-the-clock' bombing offensive, the British by night and the Americans by day. But this was still a long way off. It was a good six months after the Japanese attack on Pearl Harbor on the morning of 7 December 1941 that the first USAAF bomber crews were sent across the English Channel in borrowed RAF twin-engined Douglas Bostons to attack targets in occupied Europe; and it was another six months before the first USAAF four-engined 'heavies' dropped their bombs on Germany proper.

The target of the Americans' historic daylight raid of 27 January 1943 was the North Sea naval port of Wilhelmshaven – protected by the same hornet's nest of defending fighters that had mauled the RAF's Wellingtons so savagely back in December 1939. This time only one of the 55-strong attacking force of B-17s was brought down (although 32 more suffered damage to varying degrees).

It seemed at first as if the USAAF's faith in the ability of compact bomber formations to protect themselves against fighter attack had been fully vindicated. It was not until the Fortresses and Liberators started to venture deeper into Germany's heartland, beyond the range of the escort fighters then available, that their losses began to assume alarming proportions. These culminated in the twin attacks on Schweinfurt and Regensburg on 17 August 1943, when no fewer than 60 B-17s were brought down and nearly three times that number damaged.

A second strike against Schweinfurt less than two months later cost another 60 Fortresses, plus a further 145 damaged. Casualty rates such as these – approaching 25 per cent – meant that the daylight battle for the Reich still hung very much in the balance. The Luftwaffe's fighter and flak defences were demonstrating that, deep inside German airspace, US 'heavies' were almost as vulnerable as Bomber Command's twin-engined

The Eighth Air Force paid heavily for its early unescorted raids deep into Germany. The 100th BG's B-17F *ALICE FROM DALLAS* was just one of 60 Flying Fortresses lost on the Schweinfurt-Regensburg mission of 17 August 1943

types had been when attacking the outer edges of Hitler's domain four years previously.

But while Dr Josef Goebbels propaganda ministry was gleefully trumpeting the news of each success in the air, cooler and more professional minds could already appreciate the inherent danger posed by the Eighth Air Force's steadily growing strength. Even *before* second Schweinfurt, one relatively junior Luftwaffe officer realised, with remarkable prescience, that the Americans' inexorable build-up of power had to be disrupted before it became overwhelming – and that such disruption could only be achieved by radical measures.

KORNATZKI - *STURM* VISIONARY

The son of an army general, Hans-Günter von Kornatzki had been born in Liegnitz, Lower Silesia, on 22 June 1906. He joined the *Reichswehr* (inter-war German army) aged 21, and subsequently volunteered for flying training. Graduating from the *Jagdschule* Werneuchen in the spring of 1934, his first posting was as adjutant to I./JG 132 – the premier, and,

The man who saw the writing on the wall, Major Hans-Günter von Kornatzki was the 'Father of the *Sturm* Idea'

at that time, *only Jagdgruppe* in the then still covert Luftwaffe. The following year Oberleutnant von Kornatzki was transferred to the newly forming II./JG 132. Promoted to hauptmann in 1936, he was given command of one of five *ad hoc* ground-attack units set up at the time of the Munich crisis (see *Osprey Elite Units 13 – Luftwaffe Schlachtgruppen*).

Although the outbreak of war found Hauptmann von Kornatzki tasked with establishing new Bf 109-equipped *Jagdgruppe* II./JG 52 (see *Osprey Elite Units 15 - Jagdgeschwader 52* for further details), it was only a matter of weeks before he took up the first of a series of staff appointments. These would ultimately lead to his joining the staff of the *General der Jagdflieger*, Generalmajor Adolf Galland, on 24 September 1943.

By now having himself risen to the rank of major, von Kornatzki knew Galland of old, and lost little time in outlining his revolutionary proposals to the *General der Jagdflieger*. He conceded that Luftwaffe fighter units presently operating in the defence of the Reich were exacting a steady, and at times enormous, toll on the US 'heavies'. But what was really needed, he argued, was one major blow, or a series of major blows, designed to knock whole bomber formations out of the sky. Kornatzki believed that the Americans would be unable to ignore such losses, thus placing their entire daylight bombing strategy in jeopardy.

The best way to achieve the desired result, von Kornatzki continued, would be by creating units of 'specially trained volunteers, flying heavily armed and armoured fighters, who would be willing to get in close to the enemy, in tight formation, before opening massed fire at the shortest possible range, and who – if all else failed – would be prepared to ram their opponents'. Galland was reportedly taken by the idea and immediately authorised von Kornatzki to set up an experimental *Staffel* of what he termed *Rammjäger*.

Early in October 1943 officers toured fighter bases and schools in Germany and the occupied territories calling for volunteers. Although the response was not overwhelming, more than the required number came forward to form a single *Staffel*.

Major von Kornatzki interviewed each of the prospective candidates in his Berlin office. He explained the principles behind the unit's formation and spelled out what would be expected of its members. While not playing down the risks involved, he stressed that the *Staffel* was *not* a suicide unit (the term 'kamikaze' had not yet entered common usage). Ramming would only be used as a last resort, and then not as a deliberate act of self-immolation. Rather, the pilot would be expected to aim his heavily armoured fighter at the bomber's relatively vulnerable tail unit. The loss of, or even severe damage to, the enemy bomber's tail control surfaces would almost certainly result in its going down, while the attacker stood every chance of survival in his armour-encased cockpit.

Kornatzki likened his *Staffel* to the infantry's *Sturmtruppen*, or shock-troops – small detachments that went in ahead of the main attack to break up and demoralise the enemy. This was exactly the role he envisaged for his fighters – to blow a huge hole in the tight phalanx of bombers, causing chaos and confusion among the rigidly structured boxes, thus making them an easier target for the *Jagdgruppen* following in their wake.

The analogy obviously struck a chord in official circles too, as witness this entry in the war diary of I. *Jagdkorps*, dated 19 October 1943;

'With immediate effect, *Sturmstaffel* 1 to be activated via the proper channels for a provisionary period of six months.'

UNIT FORMATION

The 16 pilots (some sources list 18 names) selected by Major von Kornatzki at the Berlin interviews were ordered to report to Achmer airfield, near Osnabrück. They were a mixed bunch – combat veterans from both bomber and fighter units, flying instructors and newly qualified trainees. Their reasons for volunteering for the *Staffel* were as varied as their backgrounds. A similar number would join in the weeks to come, bringing *Sturmstaffel* 1's full pilot roster up to some three-dozen.

Among the latter arriving at Achmer in early November was the recently promoted Major Erwin Bacsila. Only four years younger than von Kornatzki, Bacsila had been born in Budapest in 1910 in the days of the Austro-Hungarian Empire. After graduating from the Austrian military academy between the wars, he subsequently joined Austria's fledgling air arm. Upon the *Anschluss* (annexation of Austria by Germany), Bacsila was transferred to the Luftwaffe. The outbreak of war found him as an oberleutnant serving in the Polish campaign with the Bf 109-equipped II./ZG 1 (JGr. 101).

Unlike von Kornatzki, Bacsila would remain on operations (despite his advancing years), subsequently flying with both JGs 52 and 77 in Russia and North Africa. Shortly after his 14th victory of the war (a Spitfire claimed over Agedabia on 13 December 1942), Hauptmann Bacsila was

Major von Kornatzki was ably assisted in setting up the first experimental *Sturm* unit by fighter pilot Major Erwin Bacsila

brought down behind enemy lines by British anti-aircraft fire, but he was able to make his way back to friendly territory on foot.

Following the evacuation of Tunisia, Erwin Bacsila returned to the Russian front, and it was from here that he volunteered his services for *Sturmstaffel* 1. His maturity and wealth of operational experience made him the ideal right-hand man for von Kornatzki as, together, the two majors set about the task of preparing the volunteers for what lay ahead.

Achmer proved to be the perfect location for the job, as the test field, situated some 7.5 miles (12 km) north-west of Osnabrück, played an important role in the development of Luftwaffe aircraft and weaponry during the war. Twelve months hence it would be home to the Messerschmitt Me 262s of the famous *Kommando* Nowotny (see Osprey *Aircraft of the Aces 17 – German Jet Aces of World War 2*).

The Luftwaffe's usual training of pilots for defence of the Reich duties was at times rudimentary in the extreme. Here, a white-capped oberleutnant uses models to demonstrate a frontal attack on a trio of Fortresses. So much for theory . . .

. . . the reality was somewhat different. Here 92nd BG B-17s parade majestically across the sky, while escorting fighters keep watch overhead

The two starboard 20 mm MG 151/20 wing cannon of a standard Fw 190A-6

Among the current occupants was *Erprobungskommando* 25. This experimental unit's remit was the 'development and testing of special weapons to combat four-engined bombers'. Surrounded by cannon-armed Bf 110s and Me 410s, plus Bf 109s equipped with underwing rocket tubes, the pilots of *Sturmstaffel* 1 could not have been in better company.

Their own aircraft arrived in the shape of a dozen Focke-Wulf Fw 190A-6s. These were apparently standard six-gun models (two fuselage-mounted 7.9 mm MG 17 machine guns and four 20 mm MG 151/20 wing cannon) which the *Staffel* – with the help of Focke-Wulf technicians but, allegedly, without the prior knowledge or approval of the

As well as the chamfered-edge slab of external armour plate (just visible at lower left), early *Sturm* machines were fitted with 30 mm armoured glass panels on either side of the cockpit canopy. But these 'blinkers' (or 'blinders'), as they quickly became known, were not universally popular. They severely restricted lateral vision, and many pilots had them removed

General der Jagdflieger – proceeded to modify by adding 30 mm 'Thorax' armoured glass to the windscreen quarterlights and 5 mm thick external armour plating to the sides of the cockpit.

A further refinement was the fitting of 30 mm armoured glass panels (in fairly primitive wooden frames) to either side of the sliding cockpit canopy. Quickly dubbed 'blinkers' (or 'blinders'), these panels were not universally popular. As their nickname implies, their presence seriously impaired the excellent all-round visibility for which the Fw 190 was renowned, and the problem only became worse at altitude when ice quickly built up between the panes and obscured lateral vision altogether!

Designed to protect the pilot from 0.5-in (12.7 mm) machine gun fire (the calibre of the Brownings which constituted the US 'heavies'' defensive armament), the conspicuous slabs of armoured glass and steel plate were said to be good for morale. But many pilots preferred to take their chances, willingly sacrificing the extra protection for unrestricted visibility by having the 'blinkers' removed from their machines.

The closing weeks of 1943 were spent allowing pilots to get the 'feel' of their new mounts. The added weight of armour had a marked effect on the performance of the A-6, or *Sturmjäger*, as it was dubbed. As a result, the two fuselage machine guns were removed on most machines and the muzzle troughs faired over. Unsurprisingly, it was those members of *Sturmstaffel* 1 who had previously flown ops on fighters who were among the first to master the foibles of the heavyweight Focke-Wulfs, although as

Unteroffizier Werner Peinemann of *Sturmstaffel* 1 sits in the cockpit of his Fw 190, whilst a mechanic rests on the 50 mm plate of strengthened frontal-plate glass. This aircraft also has 30 mm armoured glass quarter and side panels. Wounded in action on 4 March 1944, Peinemann joined 11./JG 3 upon his recovery two months later. He then transferred to 7.(*Sturm*)/JG 4 on 21 August 1944 and was killed when his fighter crashed on take-off on 28 September. Peinemann had a solitary victory credit to his name at the time of his death

one put it, 'I had my throttle arm through the firewall up to the elbow before I could persuade the beast even to leave the ground!'

Soon, however, all pilots were proficient enough to start practising the tactics they were to employ in battle. Unlike the head-on attacks pioneered by JG 2 (see *Osprey Aviation Elite Units 1 – Jagdgeschwader 2 'Richthofen'* for further details) when tackling US bombers over France in 1942 – the infamous 'twelve-o'clock-high' interception – von Kornatzki's plan was for the *Staffel*, flying in close arrowhead formation, to approach the enemy bombers from directly astern. The additional armour bolted to their aircraft would offer them some protection from the defensive fire that the bombers' tail, ball, waist and upper gunners would undoubtedly be throwing at them. But there was another hazard.

If an action were to take place within enemy fighter range, the cumbersome *Sturmjäger* – in precise formation, sights set on the bombers

On 17 November 1943 Luftwaffe C-in-C Hermann Göring, accompanied by *General der Jagdflieger* Adolf Galland (left), paid an official visit to Achmer. After inspecting the ranks of Hauptmann Horst Geyer's Ekdo 25 . . .

. . . the *Reichsmarschall* turned his attention to the pilots of *Sturmstaffel* 1. Here, he chats to *Staffelkapitän* Major Hans-Günter von Kornatzki

With his hand upon von Kornatzki's shoulder, Göring wishes him and his *Staffel* every success. On the *Kapitän's* left are Major Bacsila, Oberleutnant Ottmar Zehart and Leutnant Hans-Georg Elser. Note the extensive use of camouflage netting to disguise the buildings in the background

they were overhauling – would themselves be wide open to attack. Under such circumstances the *Staffel* would need a high-altitude escort of its own to keep enemy fighters off its back.

It was during this working up, on 17 November 1943, that Luftwaffe C-in-C *Reichsmarschall* Hermann Göring paid a visit of inspection to Achmer in the company of *General der Jagdflieger* Adolf Galland and a whole retinue of high-ranking officers (including former fighter *Experten* Hannes Trautloft and Günther Lützow, both now serving on Galland's staff). This was the occasion on which the affidavit quoted at the head of the chapter was duly signed by the assembled pilots of *Sturmstaffel 1*. Underlining the seriousness of their undertaking, each pilot was asked to append his last will and testament to the said document!

At the beginning of January 1944 *Sturmstaffel 1* was declared combat ready. The unit was transferred down to Dortmund, in the Ruhr, which

Early in January 1944, after completing working up, *Sturmstaffel 1* transferred to Dortmund, home of I./JG 1. Trundling through the slush, this *Gruppe's* 'Black 3' displays the unit's flamboyant markings – black and white patterned engine cowling and red aft fuselage Defence of the Reich band

Initially, the *Staffel's Sturmjäger* – here an 'unblinkered' example – also wore red aft fuselage bands. Like those at Achmer, Dortmund's hangars were well camouflaged

A combat box of B-17s heads towards Germany

was also the base of Major Rudolf-Emil Schnoor's Fw 190-equipped I./JG 1, with whom the *Staffel* was were to operate. It did not have to wait long for things to start happening.

INTO ACTION, ALMOST

On 5 January a force of 250 US 'heavies', escorted by P-38 and P-51 fighters, was despatched against the naval base of Kiel. Although both I./JG 1 and *Sturmstaffel* 1 were scrambled to intercept, only the former

made contact. Carrying out their normal frontal attacks, Schnoor's pilots claimed four B-17s for the loss of three of their own number. Failing to find the enemy, *Sturmstaffel* 1 pilots returned somewhat chastened to Dortmund to await their next opportunity. It came six days later.

On 11 January 1944 an even larger force of Eighth Air Force bombers – 663 in all, with an escort of close on 600 fighters – was sent out against a number of aviation industry targets in central Germany. Aware of the developing threat, controllers had ordered I./JG 1 and *Sturmstaffel* 1 to move from Dortmund up to Rheine, close to the Dutch border, before 0900 hrs. Remaining there at readiness, the units received the order to scramble 90 minutes later. This time the pilots of the *Sturmstaffel* stayed in contact with the more experienced I./JG 1 until the enemy was sighted. Then, as the latter positioned themselves for their usual frontal assault, which netted them a trio of B-17s, the *Sturmstaffel* closed up into the tight arrowhead formation it had been practising for weeks past and began to approach another of the bomber boxes from astern.

The attack did not produce the hoped-for result. The box was not blasted apart by the massed fire of the *Sturmjägers'* 20 mm cannon. In fact, just one Fortress was seen to go down. Even the victor, Oberleutnant Ottmar Zehart, admitted that his success owed more to luck than skill;

'I just let fly at the formation of *Viermots* in front of me. That's all.'

Nevertheless, the unlucky (and unfortunately anonymous) Boeing was a first, both for Oberleutnant Zehart – an ex-bomber pilot who had joined the *Staffel* the previous November – and for *Sturmstaffel* 1.

There is, however, some evidence to suggest that the *Staffel* carried out a second attack over an hour later, and that two more pilots, Fähnrich Manfred Derp (ex-JG 26) and Feldwebel Gerhard Marburg, also claimed a B-17 apiece on this date. To complicate matters even further, it was Major Bacsila who was *officially* credited with *Sturmstaffel* 1's first kill.

Austrian Oberleutnant Ottmar Zehart (centre), flanked here by Major Erwin Bacsila (left) and Leutnant Hans-Georg Elser (right), joined *Sturmstaffel* 1 in November 1943. Claiming the unit's first victory (a B-17) on 11 January 1944, ex-bomber pilot Zehart subsequently destroyed two B-24s with IV./JG 3 prior to joining 7.(*Sturm*)/JG 4 as its *Staffelkapitän*. Doubling his score, Zehart had six victories to his credit by the time he was posted missing in action on 27 September 1944. Elser, who joined 3./JG 2 in the spring of 1944, was posted missing in action in the Ardennes (near St Vith) on 17 December 1944. Veteran fighter pilot Erwin Bacsila survived the war with 34 confirmed and eight unconfirmed victories to his credit. He passed away on 3 March 1982 in Vienna

A line-up of fully armed and armoured A-6s shows off *Sturmstaffel* 1's newly introduced and highly distinctive black-white-black aft fuselage bands

Some of the unit's *Sturmjäger* also sported the *Staffel* badge

The typed confirmation slip, issued by the RLM in Berlin and dated 9 June 1944, clearly states that the 'Fortress II' shot down by Bacsila on 30(!) January 1944 was the 'first' aerial victory of the *Staffel*. In fact, neither von Kornatzki nor Bacsila flew many ops, and on these early missions the *Staffel* was usually led in the air by Leutnant Werner Gerth, who had previously been a member of III./JG 53 in Italy.

Whatever the true facts of 11 January, and whether they had lost one B-17 or three to the *Sturmjäger*, it would appear that the Americans remained blissfully unaware of the fact that they had been subjected to a revolutionary new method of attack.

There followed more than a fortnight of bad weather. With the Eighth Air Force restricting itself to operations mainly over France, the *Staffel* utilised the time to put in some more – demonstrably much needed – practice. Perhaps inspired by the striking black-and-white striped and

checkerboard cowlings of I./JG 1's Focke-Wulfs, it was around this time too that *Sturmstaffel* 1 adopted its distinctive black-and-white rear fuselage bands. A unit badge was also introduced, this consisting of a mailed fist clutching a stylised lightning bolt against a cloud background.

After an abortive attempt to intercept a raid on Frankfurt on 29 January, I./JG 1 and the *Sturmstaffel* were sent up again 24 hours later, and this time contact was made. *Sturmstaffel* 1 closed in on a formation of B-24s which were part of a 150-strong force attacking Hannover. Two of the Liberators were brought down. Unteroffizier Willi Maximowitz accounted for his with cannon fire, but Unteroffizier Hermann Wahlfeld's chosen victim seemed impervious to shell or shot.

With the range diminishing rapidly, Wahlfeld remained true to the *Sturm* code and rammed the heavy bomber now filling his sights. His escape unscathed by parachute and subsequent return to Dortmund was a greater morale booster for the *Staffel* than any amount of armour plating. The two B-24s were firsts for both NCO pilots, and tally neatly with the two losses admitted by the Eighth Air Force – both the 93rd and 445th Bomb Groups each lost a Liberator on this raid.

It was during this same mission that Major Bacsila was curiously

Major Erwin Bacsila (left) smiles for the camera with his Fw 190A-6 'White 7' following the completion of an early *Sturmstaffel* 1 mission from Dortmund in mid-January 1944

Unteroffizier Hermann Wahlfeld proved his commitment to the *Sturmflieger's* creed by ramming a B-24 on 30 January 1944. He succeeded in baling out of his shattered Fw 190 without so much as a scratch

19

Gefreiter Rudolf Pancherz joined *Sturmstaffel* 1 soon after the unit was formed, but was subsequently transferred to 3./JG 11 in late January 1944. Having claimed one victory with the latter unit, he was killed in a mid-air collision with another pilot from his *Staffel* on 3 March 1944

Ex-7./*Jagdgruppe Ost* instructor Unteroffizier Heinz von Neuenstein became one of *Sturmstaffel* 1's first losses when he was killed in action east of Hannover on 30 January 1944

A frontline fighter pilot since 1940, Wolfgang Kosse had been demoted from hauptmann to flieger following an unauthorised flight that went wrong whilst serving with JG 5 in 1943. This photograph of Flieger Kosse was taken soon after he joined *Sturmstaffel* 1

credited with the *Staffel's* first 'official' aerial victory. But the identification of Bacsila's victim as a 'Fortress II' would seem to suggest that he had stuck closer to the Fw 190s of I./JG 1, who had engaged the much larger formation of B-17s targeting Brunswick.

30 January also saw *Sturmstaffel* 1's first losses when Fähnrich Derp and Unteroffizier Heinz von Neuenstein (an ex-flying instructor) were both killed in action east of Hannover. Two other pilots were wounded and forced to take to their parachutes. In addition, four more machines are believed to have been completely written-off and a further six damaged. The three victories had been dearly bought.

These material losses had still not been made good by the time the *Staffel* next went up against the enemy. With little more than six Focke-Wulfs currently serviceable, there was no chance of Major von Kornatzki's 'decisive blow' being delivered on 10 February when *Sturmstaffel* 1 again accompanied I./JG 1, first to Rheine, and then into action against another raid by the Eighth Air Force on Brunswick. In the event, just one victory was added to the *Staffel's* scoreboard – a B-17 downed by Oberfähnrich Heinz Steffen not far from Rheine itself.

Twenty-four hours later Steffen claimed his second Fortress when the *Staffel* was scrambled on its own for the first time. Another of the B-17 force sent to attack Frankfurt on 11 February was credited to Flieger Wolfgang Kosse.

Flieger was the lowest rank in the Luftwaffe, the equivalent of AC2 or Private Second Class, and very few flieger were fighter pilots – unless, that is, they had been demoted from a higher rank, which is exactly what had happened to Wolfgang Kosse.

Kosse had claimed his first four kills while flying as a leutnant with JG 26 during the invasion of France and the Low Countries in May-June 1940. He added a brace of Hurricanes during the Battle of Britain as *Staffelkapitän* of 5./JG 26, and was credited with five further RAF victories during the cross-Channel skirmishing of 1941-42. After attending a gunnery course, the now Oberleutnant Kosse was transferred to JG 5 in Norway. Here, he captained 1. *Staffel*, apparently went on to claim a further six kills, and was promoted to hauptmann. Then something happened.

A post-war account claims that he performed an unauthorised flight and damaged an aircraft, although this incident was recorded in the unit history simply as an 'abuse of powers of authority'. On 30 November 1943 Kosse was immediately demoted to flieger and sentenced to nine months imprisonment, the latter then commuted to probationary frontline service. Kosse presumably regarded volunteering for the *Sturmstaffel* as a means of rehabilitating himself, and his 18th kill – the B-17 of 11 February – was the first step on the long road back.

Ten days were to pass before the *Staffel* next engaged the US 'heavies'. On 21 February, 24 hours into the Eighth's 'Big Week' offensive, some

Standing on the rain-soaked apron at Dortmund in early February 1944, the pilots of *Sturmstaffel* 1 prepare for an inspection. Indentifiable in this line-up are, from left to right, Oberleutnant Ottmar Zehart, Leutnant Hans-Georg Elser, Lt Friedrich Dammann, unknown, Feldwebel Gerhard Marburg, Unteroffizier Kurt Röhrich, Unteroffizier Werner Peinemann and Gefreiter Gerhard Vivroux

800 bombers, escorted by nearly 700 fighters, struck at Luftwaffe airfields and other targets in northwest Germany.

Again operating independently, *Sturmstaffel* 1 claimed two B-17s – one each for Feldwebel Gerhard Marburg and Unteroffizier Kurt Röhrich. The former was also credited with a *Herausschuss*. This term literally meant 'shooting out', whereby a heavy bomber had been damaged to such an extent that it was forced to abandon the safety of its combat box and become a lone straggler – easy pickings for any roving Luftwaffe fighter.

But these successes had cost the *Staffel* two more fatalities. Unteroffizier Erich Lambertus (who had transferred in from JG 26 only the previous month) and Unteroffizier Walter Köst were both shot down near Lübeck, on the Baltic coast, in two of the *Staffel's* new Fw 190A-7s.

The *Staffel's* activities were already beginning to attract attention. This still from a newsreel shot at Salzwedel in March 1944 shows Feldwebel Gerhard Marburg (left) and Unteroffizier Kurt Röhrich deep in conversation with one of the groundcrew

Far left
One of *Sturmstaffel* 1's earliest volunteers, Unteroffizier Erich Lambertus had joined the unit from 2./JG 26 on 19 January 1944. He was killed in action flying Fw 190A-7 'White 3' over Lübeck on 21 February

Left
Unteroffizier Walter Köst was also killed in action on 21 February 1944, being hit over Sundern by defensive fire from one of the B-17s he had attempted to shoot down

The Fw 190A-7 boasted a number of technical and mechanical improvements over the A-6, as well as four wing-mounted 20 mm cannon augmented by a pair of fuselage-mounted MG 131 13 mm machine guns

Sturmstaffel 1 shared Salzwedel with IV./JG 3, one of whose Bf 109Gs may just be made out in the background at far left

This latest variant from the Focke-Wulf stable differed from the previous A-6 model primarily by having its two 7.9 mm MG 17 fuselage machine guns replaced by heavier 13 mm MG 131s. But this upgrading was fairly academic as far as the *Sturmstaffel* was concerned, as the fuselage armament was usually removed anyway.

On 22 February the Eighth Air Force turned its attention from airfields to aircraft factories, but severe weather conditions over northwest Europe resulted in the majority of the bombers either aborting or being recalled. Some 38 B-17s were lost in action nonetheless, one going down to the guns of the *Staffelführer* Leutnant Werner Gerth.

Four days later *Sturmstaffel* 1 ended its brief association with I./JG 1 when its ten serviceable machines were ordered to transfer to Salzwedel – an airfield approximately midway between Hamburg and Berlin. The Bf 109G-6s of IV./JG 3 'Udet' had also transferred in to Salzwedel (from Venlo, in Holland) on this same 26 February. Commanded as from this

Major Friedrich-Karl Müller, *Gruppenkommandeur* of IV./JG 3, is seen here wearing the Oak Leaves that he was awarded for claiming 100 victories while serving as *Staffelkapitän* of I./JG 53 on the Russian front

date by Major Friedrich-Karl Müller, IV./JG 3 had only recently been assigned to Defence of the Reich duties after service in Sicily and Italy during the latter half of 1943. The new base was to bring a change of fortunes for both IV./JG 3 and *Sturmstaffel* 1.

After an unsuccessful first attempt to attack Berlin on 3 March 1944 (which was thwarted by bad weather), the Eighth Air Force had marginally better luck under similar conditions the following day when a single combat wing of 30 B-17s managed to get through to the German capital. Five of this small attacking force – the first US aircraft to bomb Berlin – were lost. One was claimed by a pilot of IV./JG 3 and two were credited to the *Sturmstaffel*.

Having scrambled from Salzwedel at about 1230 hrs, and spent the next hour searching, the *Staffel* finally located the bomber formation over Neuruppin, some 37 miles (60 km) to the northwest of the capital. A stern attack to within a few feet of the rearmost machines sent two of the B-17s

Sturmstaffel 1's Unteroffizier Gerhard Vivroux, Unteroffizier Hermann Wahlfeld, Major Erwin Bacsila (wearing in a highly prized USAAF flying jacket) and Feldwebel Werner Peinemann pose for a photo just prior to the 4 March mission in defence of Berlin. Vivroux downed a B-17 during this mission and Wahlfeld got two, but Peinemann was shot down and wounded

down within seconds of each other. One was a first for Unteroffizier Gerhard Vivroux, while the other was victory number two for Feldwebel Hermann Wahlfeld who, on this occasion, did not have to resort to ramming! The *Staffel's* sole casualty was Feldwebel Werner Peinemann, shot down wounded between Neuruppin and Salzwedel.

SUCCESS IN DEFENCE OF BERLIN

Forty-eight hours later a third attempt at 'Big B', as Berlin had promptly been christened by the US bomber crews, was an altogether different story. The Eighth Air Force's Mission No 250 of 6 March 1944 comprised 730 B-17s and B-24s, accompanied by 800 escort fighters. This time not even the heavy cloud cover was going to be able to protect the capital of Hitler's Reich. But the Luftwaffe, alerted by the earlier aborted raids, had been given plenty of time to gather its defences. A total of 18 *Jagdgruppen*, three *Zerstörergruppen*, four *Nachtjagdgruppen* and sundry lesser units awaited the approaching Americans.

Into this aerial arena, crowded with some 2,000 combat aircraft, friend an foe alike, *Sturmstaffel* 1 was able to despatch just seven Fw 190s. Their contribution might seem miniscule, but between them the seven *Sturmjäger* would be credited with seven B-17s destroyed – their greatest success to date, and a figure which alone represented ten per cent of Mission No 250's total heavy bomber losses!

It had been approximately 1130 hrs when the seven Focke-Wulfs were scrambled from Salzwedel in the company of IV./JG 3's Bf 109s. Climbing steadily, they set course south-eastwards for the Magdeburg area, 62 miles (100 km) distant, where they were to rendezvous with other fighter units at an altitude of 26,000 ft (7,900 m). All went to plan, and

Some 15 Fw 190s (most of them A-7s) of *Sturmstaffel* 1 sit on the ramp outside the hangar at Salzwedel in early March 1944. Most are carrying drop tanks, and they all seem to feature the black-white-black fuselage identification bands of the *Sturmstaffel*

soon the van of the huge US bomber stream was sighted approaching from the direction of Brunswick.

In the face of such overwhelming enemy strength it was obviously impossible to use *Sturmstaffel* 1's seven Fw 190s in the role originally envisaged for them by von Kornatzki – 'to make the initial pass, smash a breach in the enemy's defences and cause disruption among his ranks'. Instead, the twin-engined Messerschmitts went in first with heavy cannons and rockets, followed by the single-seat fighters. Then it was the *Sturmjägers'* turn.

Three B-17s fell to their first onslaught, all logged as going down at 1235 hrs – one apiece for Leutnant Gerhard Dost and Unteroffizier Kurt Röhrich, and an *Herausschuss* for Unteroffizier Willi Maximowitz. Two more Fortresses were then claimed by Oberleutnant Ottmar Zehart and Unteroffizier Hermann Wahlfeld, and a final brace were credited to Leutnant Werner Gerth, the last shot down at 1408 hrs.

A classic *Herausschuss* as a 1st Bomb Division B-17 drops away with its starboard outer engine on fire

The *Staffel's* sole casualty was Gerhard Dost who, after claiming his first victory in the initial pass, was last seen on the tail of a straggling B-17. Intent on adding a second kill to his scoreboard, he did not spot the pair of P-51s diving to the bomber's aid until it was too late. He turned into his attackers, but the heavy *Sturmjäger* (which only now jettisoned its drop tank) was no match for the two Mustangs. The American fighters circled Dost's machine, forcing it to lose altitude in a tight spiral. At 5000 ft (1500 m) it stalled out while trying to turn inside the P-51s and crashed into the ground not far from Salzwedel. Neither American pilot had been able to get in a single shot at Dost's 'White 20' during the steep, wildly gyrating 400 mph (645 km/h) chase.

The survivor from a 91st BG Fortress brought down north of Magdeburg during this action has described being attacked from astern by a trio of Fw 190s, one of which lost height a little, before climbing 'relentlessly' straight towards the B-17 and knocking its starboard tailplane off in the resulting collision. There is no mention of a deliberate ramming attack in the Luftwaffe's list of kills, but it seems almost certain that this incident involved an aircraft of *Sturmstaffel* 1. The only clue to the pilot's identity is afforded by the time of the bomber's loss – given as 'approximately 1250 hrs' – which would best tie in with Ottmar Zehart's claim of 1255 hrs.

6 March 1944 was also the most successful day to date for the pilots of IV./JG 3, who claimed 13 enemy aircraft without loss to themselves. Forty-eight hours later, when the Eighth Air Force again struck at Berlin, the unit was credited with another dozen victories, although this time one pilot was killed and two wounded. The *Sturmstaffel's* sole success on 8 March was a single B-17 downed by Leutnant Richard Franz (to add to his one B-17 claimed during his earlier service with JG 77 in Italy).

Leutnant Gerhard Dost scored his first victory over a B-17 on 6 March, but he was in turn set upon by escorting P-51Bs and killed when his heavy *Sturmjäger* stalled and crashed after Dost had tried to turn inside his attackers

'White 1' and '2' sit out on a rather damp apron in front of their Salzwedel hangar as they are readied for another mission. Although the former was the *Kapitän's* assigned machine . . .

. . . Major von Kornatzki normally flew 'White 20', seen here basking in the early spring sunshine. Note what appears to be a Gotha Go 242 transport glider in the background left

Severe weather largely protected Berlin from another raid on 9 March, but it also kept the *Staffel* anchored firmly to the ground at Salzwedel. The bad weather would continue for another fortnight, and it was not until 23 March that the *Sturmjäger* next saw action. Although conditions were still far from good, *Sturmstaffel* 1, again in the company of IV./JG 3, was scrambled against US 'heavies' raiding targets in northwest Germany. After an hour's searching, they found a formation of bombers north of the Ruhr and brought down six of their number (three of them *Herausschüsse*) in the space of ten minutes.

Four of the victors – Kasse, Maximowitz, Röhrich and Vivroux – already had *Sturm* kills under their belts, but two of the *Herausschüsse* were firsts, one going to Friedrich Dammann and the other to Major

Reflecting on a close encounter with a P-51B, Unteroffizier Hermann Wahlfeld sits in the cockpit of his Fw 190, its starboard 'blinker' panel shattered by a 0.50-in machine gun round. Although Wahlfeld's luck held out on this occasion, it deserted him on 23 March 1944 when he was shot down and killed near Lippstadt. His tally stood at three victories at the time of his death

Hans-Günter Kornatzki (who was making one of his rare operational flights on this date), which took his tally of wartime victories to five.

The *Staffel* did not escape without loss, however. Unteroffizier Hermann Wahlfeld, who had carried out the first recorded ramming attack, was shot down and killed near Lippstadt. Feldwebel Otto Weissenberger suffered a similar fate west of Bocholt. The latter, an early volunteer, had not scored while with the *Staffel*, although he had previously served with JG 5 in the far north alongside his elder brother, Theodor, who was by this time an Oak Leaves-wearing *Experte* with 148 victories to his name. The third casualty was Unteroffizier Willi Maximowitz, forced to bale out wounded over Wuppertal.

Unteroffizier Willi Maximowitz (left) and Gefreiter Gerhard Vivroux pose with Fw 190A-6 'White 2' at Dortmund in early 1944. Note the *Sturmstaffel* 1 emblem adorning the fighter's nose and the 'blinkers' fitted to its canopy

Further proof that the Panzerglas 'blinkers' did indeed work in combat. Unteroffizier Willi Maximowitz's 'White 10' has been struck in the fuselage and cockpit by at least two machine gun rounds

Once again the weather clamped down, resulting in another long period of inactivity until the *Staffel's* next engagement on 8 April. The Eighth Air Force was still targeting Luftwaffe airfields and installations in northwest Germany, and *Sturmstaffel* 1 (together with IV./JG 3) was part of the force sent up against the bombers. Making contact with a formation of B-24s west of Brunswick, four of the more experienced pilots were able to add to their growing list of victories, claiming a trio of Liberators and an errant Fortress. But three others were not so fortunate. Unteroffiziere Karl Rohde and Walter Kukuk, neither of whom had yet scored, and Leutnant Friedrich Dammann, who had been credited with a B-17 *Herausschuss* 16 days earlier, all went down north of Brunswick.

The following day's single success was a B-24, which Flieger Wolfgang Kosse was able to add to the two B-17s he had already claimed as an ongoing part of his rehabilitation process. Then, on 11 April, it was back to multiple kills – nine in all, including the *Staffel's* first US fighter.

Once again, the Eighth Air Force's targets were Germany's airfields and aircraft factories. Having scrambled from Salzwedel shortly after 1000 hrs (together with IV./JG 3 as usual),

The *Staffel's* first fighter kill was a P-47D Thunderbolt downed on 11 April 1944. The Ninth Air Force's 362nd FG, to which the machine shown here belonged, was up that day, and lost one of the seven P-47s reported missing

Austrian Unteroffizier Kurt Röhrich was the first pilot to claim a fighter destroyed for *Sturmstaffel* 1 when he downed a P-47D on 11 April. He had been credited with 12 victories by the time of his death on 19 July

Ex-JG 5 pilot Leutnant Rudolf Metz was amongst the ranks of *Sturmstaffel* 1's victorious pilots on 11 April, when the unit claimed five B-24s (one *Herausschuss*) over Hildesheim in just 60 seconds. Serving with 11./JG 3 between 9 May and 30 June, Metz was then posted to II.(*Sturm*)/JG 4. Having increased his tally to ten victories, he was killed in action while serving with 6.(*Sturm*)/JG 4 on 6 October 1944

Sturmstaffel 1 was vectored towards a formation of some 50 B-24s in the Hildesheim area. Five Liberators went down in the first attack timed at 1115 hrs – one each for Metz, Müller, Röhrich (*Herausschuss*), Marburg and Gerth. The latter pair claimed another B-24 apiece in a second pass only minutes later. It was Unteroffizier Kurt Röhrich who also got a P-47 Thunderbolt, which was the first enemy fighter to fall to the *Staffel*.

After refuelling and re-arming back at Salzwedel, another mission was flown early in the afternoon which resulted in a B-17 for Unteroffizier Gerhard Vivroux. Nine victories for no casualties was by far *Sturmstaffel* 1's best performance to date. The same applied to IV./JG 3, which was credited with no fewer than 25 enemy aircraft (two-dozen B-17s and a single P-38) for one pilot killed and one wounded in combat.

After the success of 11 April, the claim for just five B-17s without loss two days later might appear almost anti-climactic. But the clinical way in which this quintet had been scythed from a formation of some 150 Fortresses west of Schweinfurt, all within the space of a minute, was a telling demonstration of *Sturm* tactics. Three of the bombers fell to old hands, being the fourth, fifth and sixth victories for Gerhard Vivroux,

31

Armourers hastily attend to the reloading of one of the wing-mounted 20 mm MG 151/20 cannon fitted to a *Sturmstaffel* 1 Fw 190A-7 at Salzwedel in early April 1944. The fighter's spinner and cowling are streaked with engine fluid and gun muzzle deposits

Siegfried Müller and Werner Gerth, respectively. The remaining two, both *Herausschüsse*, were firsts for Unteroffiziere Karl-Heinz Schmidt and Heinrich Fink.

Twenty-four hours later the unfortunate Unteroffizier Fink was to become the *Staffel's* eleventh, and final, combat fatality when shot down in unknown circumstances in the Stuttgart area.

OFFICIAL RECOGNITION

Sturmstaffel 1 was now rapidly approaching the end of its six-month trial period. The unit's performance, especially of late, had obviously impressed the upper hierarchy, for on 15 April *General der Jagdflieger* Adolf Galland visited Salzwedel not only to congratulate von Kornatzki and his pilots, but also – and perhaps more importantly – to announce that IV./JG 3 had been selected to become the Luftwaffe's first official *Sturmgruppe!*

The General's plans called for IV./JG 3 to convert from its Bf 109G-6s to Fw 190A *Sturmjäger* – remaining operational throughout – and to incorporate *Sturmstaffel* 1 into its ranks as a new 11.(*Sturm*)/JG 3. But for the next fortnight, while orders were being cut and details finalised, *Sturmstaffel* 1 would continue to operate under its original designation.

On 18 April the Eighth Air Force returned to aviation industry targets in the Greater Berlin area. This time the bad weather, which seemed an almost permanent feature of Berlin ops during this period, worked against the defenders. Although IV./JG 3 and the *Sturmstaffel* scrambled from Salzwedel safely enough, they were unable to rendezvous with other units as planned. *Sturmstaffel* 1 was the first to find and engage a formation of B-17s, escorted by fighters, some 37 miles (60 km) to the west of the

capital. Kurt Röhrich and Wolfgang Kosse – the latter now elevated to the rank of gefreiter (AC1 or PFC) – were credited with a Fortress each, while Oberfeldwebel Gerhard Marburg was able to bring down a P-51 in a separate action 20 minutes later.

But it was the *Staffel's* swansong, on 29 April, which proved to be its finest hour. Once again the Eighth Air Force (over 600 bombers escorted by more than 800 fighters) had its sights on Berlin.

For the last time, IV./JG 3 and *Sturmstaffel* 1 lifted off from Salzwedel – in company, but as separate entities. At the rendezvous point the Bf 109s joined up with other *Jagdgruppen* before setting off for the Magdeburg area, where strong enemy forces had been reported. These were engaged by IV./JG 3 using their customary frontal attack tactics. The *Gruppe* claimed nine B-17s and five B-24s (four of the Fortresses and all five Liberators being *Herausschüsse*).

Meanwhile, the *Sturmstaffel* had found a formation of B-17s to the northeast of Brunswick. Relying on their usual stern approach, the heavily armoured *Sturmjäger* bored in. The next five or six minutes were both the culmination of *Sturmstaffel* 1's short-lived history and the most convincing demonstration to date of Major von Kornatzki's original close-quarter concept.

Thirteen Fortresses were hacked down. As was to be expected, it was again the more experienced pilots – by now the '*Alten Hase*' (Old Hares) of *Sturm* tactics – who gained the lion's share of the successes. Both Werner Gerth and Kurt Röhrich took their *Sturm* scores to eight, the former with a double victory. Wolfgang Kosse also claimed a brace (both of them *Herausschüsse*) in this action, but two of the three remaining *Herausschüsse* were firsts for Unteroffiziere Helmut Keune and Oskar Bösch.

On 24 April *Sturmstaffel* 1 claimed no fewer than seven B-17 *Herausschüsse* in the Munich area. Could the 384th BG's *BOOBY TRAP*, seen here on her belly in the shadow of the Alps, perhaps have been one of them?

Unteroffizier Oskar Bösch's first victory was a B-17 *Herausschuss* northeast of Brunswick on 29 April 1944 . . .

Throughout its six-month operational career, the *Staffel* had welcomed a small but steady stream of new volunteers to its ranks. Oskar Bösch had been one of the last to reach the unit, as he explained to the Author;

'Although my travel orders directed me to report to JG 3, I volunteered instead for *Sturmstaffel* 1. A few days later I arrived at Salzwedel. As I had never flown an Fw 190 before, I was first given a short introduction and then allowed to practise four take-offs and do a few circuits.

. . . and here the victor poses (right) with his mechanic on the wing of his Fw 190A-7. Note that although the fuselage-mounted MG 131 machine guns have been removed, the barrel troughs (on top of the cowling) have not been faired over

'The next day, 29 April 1944, I took off on my first operational mission. We did not open fire until we had approached to within a few metres of the bombers. During this mission our unit shot down 22 (sic) *Viermotorige*, one of which was credited to me. As my fuel was running low I had to land at Bernburg, where my Fw 190A-7 somersaulted and I was slightly injured.'

When Oskar Bösch returned to ops nine days later, he would find himself a member of JG 3 after all, for a top secret communication from OKL (Luftwaffe High Command) HQ, dated 29 April 1944 and headed 'Activation of a *Sturmgruppe*', began with the words;

'1. <u>With immediate effect</u>
(a) <u>IV./JG 3</u> is to be <u>redesignated</u> and <u>converted</u> into
    <u>IV./(*Sturm*)/JG 3</u>
(b) and <u>*Sturmstaffel* 1</u> is to be <u>disbanded</u>.'

The document then went into administrative detail, specifying, among other points, that personnel from the disbanded *Sturmstaffel* were to be integrated into the newly created *Sturmgruppe* (the majority would, in fact, be used to establish the new 11. *Staffel*), and that IV.(*Sturm*)/JG 3 was to be re-equipped with Fw 190 *Sturm* aircraft, its Bf 109Gs being passed mainly to the other *Gruppen* of JG 3 to help make good any current shortfalls.

The pioneering, almost buccaneering, days of the all-volunteer *Sturmstaffel* were over. Major von Kornatzki's theories had been proven and accepted by those in authority. The strength of the *Sturm* force had been trebled, and it was now to form part of the regular Luftwaffe establishment. Not all welcomed the change.

The 15 pilots of *Sturmstaffel* 1 link arms for a commemorative snapshot at Salzwedel on 29 April 1944. The full line-up, from left to right is, Oberleutnant Zehart, Leutnant Elser, Leutnant Müller, Leutnant Metz, Major von Kornatzki, Leutnant Gerth, Feldwebel Röhrich, Leutnant Franz, Feldwebel Kosse, Oberfeldwebel Marburg, Feldwebel Peinemann, Unteroffizier Maximowitz, Feldwebel Groten, Unteroffizier Bösch and Unteroffizier Keune. Only three of these pilots would survive the war

IV.(*STURM*)/JG 3 – A SHAKY START

V./JG 3 had a new *Gruppenkommandeur* to oversee its transition into a frontline *Sturm* unit. In office for less than a fortnight, Hauptmann Wilhelm Moritz – a 30-year-old from the Altona district of Hamburg – had spent the early months of the war as a fighter instructor. He then held positions of command in both JGs 1 and 51 on the western and eastern fronts, before becoming a member of the *Geschwaderstab* JG 3.

Moritz was aware that a number of his pilots were not altogether happy at their enforced change of status. Why, some asked, could they not continue their provenly successful campaign against the Eighth Air Force flying frontal attacks in their cannon-armed Bf 109s? The 'honour' of being the Luftwaffe's first dedicated *Sturmgruppe* would, they argued, be better given to a unit already operating Fw 190s.

Others were concerned at being asked to sign the *Sturm* declaration. None had volunteered for the role, and the implied threat of a court martial for 'cowardice in the face of the enemy' should they return without a kill was not something to be taken lightly. They turned to members of the *Sturmstaffel* for advice.

The officer who took over command of IV./JG 3 shortly before the unit's transformation into the Luftwaffe's first *Sturmgruppe* was Hauptmann Wilhelm Moritz. He is pictured here (centre, in leather flying jacket) at a later date talking to Oberleutnant Horst Haase (back to camera), the *Kapitän* of the attached 2./JG 51

Two of IV./JG 3's rising stars at this time were Feldwebel Walther Hagenah, who had claimed a pair B-17s (bringing his score to ten) on the day Hauptmann Moritz assumed command, and would end the war flying the Me 262 with JG 7 . . .

'How many pilots had actually rammed an enemy bomber,' they asked, 'and what had happened to those who returned to base without scoring a victory?' 'Very few' and 'Absolutely nothing', were the replies. In the event most pilots of IV./JG 3 *did* sign the affidavit, but no action was taken against those who refused to do so.

Hauptmann Moritz had his own views on the subject;

'Upon call-up, every member of the Wehrmacht (German armed forces) swore an oath of allegiance in which he declared his willingness to lay down his life for his country. Any further declaration was unnecessary and superfluous.'

It is reported that Moritz personally burned those documents already signed, and there the matter rested.

Nor was the highly professional Moritz overly impressed by Majors von Kornatzki and Bacsila. The former has rightly become known as the 'Father of the *Sturm* Idea', but in Moritz's opinion, he was also more of a father figure than a commanding officer to his men. Both he and Erwin

. . . and Unteroffizier Walter Loos, pictured here with the Knight's Cross he received in April 1945 for his 38 confirmed victories, 22 of which had been four-engined bombers

A test machine displays the armament of the definitive Fw 190A-8/R2 *Sturmbock* – one inboard 20 mm MG 151/20 cannon and one outboard 30 mm MK 108 cannon in each wing (with a gun-camera window, seen here in the wing leading-edge, between the two). The destructive power of the sleeved, short-barrelled MK 108 was enormous

Bacsila, who had all the charm of a native Austrian, were well-liked, but neither had a tight grip on the reins.

In a decidedly uncomfortable meeting held to discuss the details of the *Sturmstaffel's* assimilation into IV./JG 3 (and for which *Gruppenkommandeur* Moritz had to present himself at *Staffelkapitän* von Kornatzki's HQ in deference to the latter's senior rank!), it transpired that the titular *Kapitän* had flown only nine ops during his unit's six-month campaign against the Eighth Air Force, and that he would not be able to undertake any more in the foreseeable future on account of his sinus problems. Major Bacsila was also currently *hors de combat* with a broken thumb.

Hauptmann Moritz relayed this unfortunate state of affairs to the *General der Jagdflieger*. The two majors, both well beyond the accepted ideal age for a fighter pilot, were transferred to less arduous duties. Leutnant Werner Gerth, who had led the *Sturmstaffel* in the air on so many occasions, would be appointed as *Staffelkapitän* of 11.(*Sturm*)/JG 3 on 8 May.

The *Gruppe's* conversion to Focke-Wulfs during the coming month was less contentious. In the last weeks of its existence, the *Sturmstaffel* had taken delivery of its first Fw 190A-8s. On the surface this version differed little from the earlier A-7, the modifications, such as increased fuel capacity, being mainly internal. IV.(*Sturm*)/JG 3 would come to standardise on the A-8 model, particularly the Fw 190A-8/R2 sub-variant. This had the outer pair of 20 mm MG 151/20 wing cannon replaced by 30 mm MK 108s. Known unofficially as the *Sturmbock* (Battering-ram), the Fw 190A-8/R2 became arguably the Luftwaffe's most potent piston-engined bomber-killer.

The added weight of the MK 108 cannon, plus their armour-plated ammunition magazines (in total, the R2's armour was almost 440 lb (200

kg) heavier than that fitted to the standard A-8 fighter), meant, however, that the *Sturmbock* was even more unwieldy – 'sluggish on the ailerons', according to one surviving *Sturm* pilot – if forced into a dogfight. The provision of an effective fighter escort would be more important than ever in future operations.

The *Gruppe* first scrambled in earnest on 4 May. As so often before in the recent past, the citizens of Berlin, and of the other targets scheduled for the attentions of the Eighth Air Force on this date, were safeguarded by heavy cloud. Brief contact was made with a formation of bombers somewhere to the northwest of Magdeburg, which resulted in a Bf 109 pilot of 10. *Staffel* making the unit's sole claim – the *Herausschuss* of a B-17. It was to be a very different story four days later.

8 May 1944 marked IV./JG 3's first mission as a *bona fide Sturmgruppe* (it would henceforth be referred to in all official communications as IV.(*Sturm*)/JG 3). The day also saw the *Sturmstaffel's* debut as 11.(*Sturm*)/JG 3. Hauptmann Moritz's mixed force of Bf 109s and Fw 190s lifted off from Salzwedel at about 0840 hrs as reports of another expected heavy raid began coming in. Some 500 B-17s were indeed heading for Berlin, with a slightly smaller formation of B-24s having been despatched against Brunswick. But, once again, dense layers of cloud over central Germany threw the attackers' plans into disarray.

The adverse weather conditions also hindered the 17 defending *Jagdgruppen* deployed by the Luftwaffe. After first being vectored to an assembly point in the Hamburg region, IV.(*Sturm*)/JG 3 was then ordered to fly south to intercept the approaching bombers. Shortly after 1000 hrs, they sighted several boxes of B-24s on a south-easterly course heading in the direction of Brunswick. By chance, no US escort fighters were flying close attendance on the bombers.

This well-known photograph has been variously captioned in the past as a B-24 either broken in two by a direct flak hit, or as the result of 30 mm cannon fire. The MK 108 was certainly capable of inflicting such damage

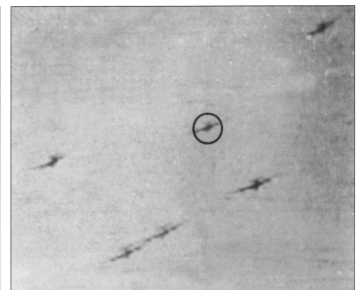

On 8 May 1944, ex-*Sturmstaffel* 1 pilot Oberfeldwebel Gerhard Marburg (above) shot down a B-24 whilst flying with IV.(*Sturm*)/JG 3. These two stills were taken from his gun-camera film, revealing the final seconds of his closure on the formation high over Germany. The USAAF lost 11 Liberators on this day. Marburg, who claimed five victories with *Sturmstaffel* 1, downed two more aircraft with IV./JG 3, before transferring to *Stab* II.(*Sturm*)/JG 4. He was killed in action on 3 September

In less than ten minutes the *Gruppe* had claimed no fewer than 19 of the Liberators. The 12 destroyed tally closely with the 11 B-24 combat losses suffered by the Americans on this mission, while the seven *Herausschüsse* may have accounted for at least some of the additional seven written-off in crash-landings back in the UK.

After returning to Salzwedel to refuel and re-arm, a second scramble was ordered shortly before noon. This resulted in the addition of five B-17s to the tally, bringing IV.(*Sturm*)/JG 3's total for the day to 24 heavy bombers! This made it by far the highest scoring *Jagdgruppe* of all those engaged on 8 May (the second most successful was credited with 'just' eight heavy bombers). The price the unit paid was one pilot killed, one wounded and five Bf 109s lost or damaged.

This Liberator is shuddering under the fire of a frontal attack. But note the *Schwarm* of Fw 190s curving round to come in astern of the formation

The action northwest of Brunswick had, at a single stroke, taken the Luftwaffe's *Sturm* campaign against the Eighth Air Force to a higher level. The large number of claims for enemy bombers shot down on this day (and there would be even higher daily totals in the months to come, particularly after the conversion of two further *Jagdgruppen* to the *Sturm* role) means that it is no longer possible in a work of this size to itemise each individual claim. Nor is it feasible always to differentiate between aircraft destroyed and those classified as *Herausschüsse*.

For a more detailed description of the various types of claims made for US heavy and medium bombers, and the number of 'points' each was worth in the Luftwaffe's somewhat convoluted awards system, see *Osprey Aircraft of the Aces 9 – Focke-Wulf 190 Aces of the Western Front* for further details.

Suffice it here to say that, on 8 May, Hauptmann Moritz began, as he intended to go on by leading his *Gruppe* from the front. He was credited with a brace of B-24s. The *Kapitän* of his 10. *Staffel*, Leutnant Hans Weik, went one better by not only claiming two of the Liberators, but also destroying a B-17 during the second mission shortly after midday. These first *Sturm* successes took their overall totals to 37 and 31 respectively. Not surprisingly, the ex-alumni of *Sturmstaffel* 1 also featured prominently on the unit's scoreboard. Four of their nine victories were doubles for Oberleutnant Ottmar Zehart and Unteroffizier Oskar Bösch.

Leutnant Hans Weik, *Staffelkapitän* of 10.(*Sturm*)/JG 3, would claim 22 four-engined bombers (out of a total score of 36) by war's end

ATTACKING GERMAN OIL PRODUCTION

Four days later, on 12 May, the Eighth Air Force switched priorities by mounting the first attack of what was to be a long-running offensive against the Third Reich's oil industry. It was a major effort, with nearly 900 heavily escorted bombers targeting refineries in central Germany and occupied Czechoslovakia. The Luftwaffe responded in kind, putting up 16 *Jagdgruppen* and three twin-engined *Zerstörergruppen*.

Once again, IV.(*Sturm*)/JG 3's performance far outstripped all others. Encountering several boxes of B-17s to the northwest of Frankfurt-on-

Main, Major Moritz's force, still composed mainly of Bf 109s, mounted two frontal attacks – one following almost immediately upon the other – which netted them 20 Fortresses in the space of just 13 minutes! The cost to the *Gruppe* was another five Messerschmitts lost or damaged. The only pilot casualty was 11. *Staffel's* Unteroffizier Gerhard Vivroux, who was wounded and baled out of his Fw 190 over Limburg, east of Koblenz.

Twenty-four hours later the Eighth's 'heavies' again set out for oil industry targets, this time in western Poland. But the previous day's clear skies had given way to thick cloud in the target area, and the bombers were diverted instead against the German Baltic ports of Stralsund and Stettin (today the Polish Szczecin). Ten of the 200+ B-17s which attacked these targets of opportunity were reported missing. Seven of that number had been brought down by IV.(*Sturm*)/JG 3, with Wilhelm Moritz and Hans Weik again among the claimants. After the engagement, Leutnant Weik was forced to belly-land his damaged Bf 109G-6 15 miles (24 km) south of Stralsund. 12. *Staffel's* Unteroffizier Oskar Fischer was less fortunate, being shot down and killed in his *Gustav* in the same region.

Fischer's 'Yellow 13' was the last Messerschmitt loss to be suffered by the *Gruppe*. The operational lull that followed – brought about by a combination of inclement weather and the Eighth Air Force turning its attention to targets in northwest occupied Europe as part of the softening-up process for the imminent invasion of Normandy – gave Moritz's pilots the opportunity to concentrate on converting to the Fw 190.

During May, in addition to the 18 Focke-Wulfs brought into the fold by *Sturmstaffel* 1, the *Gruppe* took delivery of a further 45 Fw 190A-8s. Full conversion was completed without incident, and the last half-dozen Bf 109G-6s had been passed on to other *Gruppen* within the *Geschwader* (all three of which flew Bf 109s throughout the war) by early June.

Every *Jagdgeschwader* within the Defence of the Reich organisation, and this included JG 3, was allocated a distinctive aft fuselage coloured band (or bands) as an aid to recognition in the air. Those worn by the machines of JG 3 were a plain white, and broad white bands were soon applied to all 63 Focke-Wulfs (which, perforce, meant the disappearance of the *Sturmstaffel's* 'unofficial', but decidedly more decorative, black-white-black rear fuselage stripes). On each white band, however, was stencilled the truncated black 'wavy bar' that was the standard IV. *Gruppe* symbol of the period.

In addition, the engine cowlings of most of the unit's Fw 190s were painted semi-gloss black, and this was often extended back in a stylised 'lightning flash' (sometimes edged in the *Staffel* colour) to mask the exhaust stains around the cooling louvres. As a final touch, many of the Focke-Wulfs also sported JG 3's 'Winged U' badge, which the *Geschwader* had adopted after being given the honour title 'Udet' in official commemoration of *Generaloberst* Ernst Udet, the Luftwaffe's late *Generalluftzeugmeister* (Director-General of Aircraft Procurement and Supply) who had, in fact, committed suicide back in November 1941.

But the month of May was not taken up entirely in applying fancy paint jobs. The *Gruppe* also began experimenting with the formations it would later employ to such devastating effect in Defence of the Reich operations. First, the broad massed arrowheads of anything up to two-dozen fighters, with Hauptmann Moritz and his *Gruppenstab* in the van leading all three

Looking at first glance like a line-up of standard *Sturmböcke* under a dramatically threatening sky, closer inspection reveals that each of the machines pictured here is fitted with a *'Krebsgerät'* under-fuselage, rearward-firing rocket launcher . . .

Staffeln, which were to be used during the lengthy stern approach flights to the enemy bombers. Then the splitting into individual, line-abreast *Staffeln* for the actual attack.

May also saw elements of Oberleutnant Hans Rachner's 12. *Staffel* detached to Barth, on the Baltic coast, to carry out trials with a new weapons system. The weapon in question was the same tube-launched 21 cm rocket with which IV./JG 3's Bf 109s had been equipped the previous year in Italy. There, the unit's *Gustavs* had carried a launch tube under each wing. 12. *Staffel's* Focke-Wulfs were fitted with a single fixed tube under the fuselage, arranged to fire *backwards*!

The thinking behind the so-called *'Krebsgerät'* ('Crab device') was that 12. *Staffel* would carry out a frontal attack on a bomber box. This would

. . . which is seen here more closely (albeit in silhouette) under Unteroffizier Willi Unger's 'Yellow 17' during 12. *Staffel's* trials at Barth. Note the white band and IV. *Gruppe* symbol on the machine in the background

mean their separation from the bulk of the *Gruppe* during the approach, much as *Sturmstaffel* 1 pilots had done during their early combined missions with IV./JG 3, when it was *they* who had attacked from the rear while the main body made a frontal pass. Once through the bomber formation, 12. *Staffel's* Focke-Wulfs would climb away, each firing a rocket back down at the enemy bombers as they went.

Despite the launching trials carried out over the Baltic, which were continued after 12./JG 3 was reunited back at Salzwedel, the idea proved totally impracticable and the *'Krebsgerät'* was never used on operations. One unfortunate result of the trials was the loss of Unteroffizier Johannes Staasen, whose heavy Fw 190A-8/R2, made all the more cumbersome by the underslung rocket tube, was shot down north of Barth on 16 May by a most unlikely opponent – one of a pair of roving RAF Mosquito long-range fighters.

While 12./JG 3 was struggling to master the intricacies of its rearward-firing rockets, parts of Hauptmann Moritz's other two *Staffeln* were scrambled on 19 May when the Eighth Air Force suddenly reappeared over the Reich, striking at Berlin, Brunswick and Kiel. This first all-Fw 190 mission put up by IV.(*Sturm*)/JG 3 was not an unqualified success. The Focke-Wulfs attacked one of the Berlin-bound formations near Parchim, but they were unable to penetrate the Fortresses' strong fighter escort. One or two individual pilots did manage to break through the screen of protective P-51s and a single Fortress was claimed.

Harried by the aggressive tactics of the Mustangs, many pilots were forced to land at airfields close to the capital. Those who made it back to Salzwedel were sent up for a second time. Catching the bombers on their return flight across the Baltic, they added four more B-17s to the day's score. Two NCO pilots of 11. *Staffel* were lost, one being shot down and killed north of Grönwohldshorst, on the Baltic coast, and the other making an emergency landing 25 miles (40 km) from Salzwedel, but with such severe wounds that he succumbed the following day.

On 24 May the Eighth Air Force again struck at 'Big B'. 10. and 11. *Staffeln*, together with several other units, engaged the enemy formation to the north of the capital, this time with more success. Not only were they credited with nine B-17s, they also managed to bring down three of the bombers' fighter escort – a P-38 Lightning and a pair of P-51s. One of the latter took Leutnant Werner Gerth's score to a round dozen. The *Sturmstaffeln* lost one Fw 190, whose pilot baled out uninjured.

The destruction of three US fighters was a highly creditable performance. But it was becoming increasingly clear that the ever-growing numbers of such fighters – especially P-51s – escorting the bomber streams would soon begin to pose serious problems, not just to the heavy *Sturmböcke* of IV.(*Sturm*)/JG 3, but to the defending *Jagdwaffe* as a whole.

Another of the *Gruppe's* early adversaries was the P-38 Lightning. 11.(*Sturm*)/JG 3's Unteroffizier Karl-Heinz Schmidt claimed one such machine (not from the 364th FG shown here, however) on 24 May . . .

It was at this juncture that several *Jagdgruppen* fighting on other fronts, primarily in Russia and the Mediterranean, were each stripped of one of their component *Staffeln*, which were to be transferred back to the homeland to strengthen those *Gruppen* operating in the daylight Defence of the Reich. The *Staffel* assigned to IV.(*Sturm*)/JG 3 was 2./JG 51 'Mölders', which had been serving on the eastern front since the invasion of the Soviet Union in the summer of 1941. Having only recently converted from their Fw 190s back onto Bf 109s in Russia, Oberleutnant

. . . but it was the Merlin-engined P-51 Mustang which, in the months to come, was to prove the *Sturmgruppens'* nemesis. The first USAAF fighter group to fly this long-range thoroughbred in the ETO was the Ninth Air Force's 354th FG

One-to-one against a Mustang, the heavy *Sturmbock* was at a decided disadvantage. Caught on gun-camera, this Fw 190 pilot manages to bale out. Not all would be so fortunate

Posing here in front of his Fw 190 in
Russia, Unteroffizier Klaus Neumann
was one of many 2./JG 51 pilots who
would make their mark flying *Sturm*
operations over the homeland

Horst Haase and his pilots arrived at Salzwedel in the last week of May,
where they promptly began reconverting back to Focke-Wulfs!

That last week of the month witnessed several major confrontations
between the Eighth Air Force and the defending Luftwaffe, but
IV.(*Sturm*)/JG 3's participation in these actions seems to have been very
minor indeed. On 28 May an unprecedented 1,341 'heavies', supported
and escorted by almost as many fighters of the Eighth and Ninth Air

Another ex-eastern front veteran
from JG 51, Feldwebel Konrad Bauer
would become one of the most
successful bomber-killers of the
Defence of the Reich campaign. Note
the small yellow ring (painted on the
breech cover above the aircraft's
name) which indicated that this
machine was fitted with an uprated
BMW 801D-2 engine

Forces, were despatched against oil and transportation targets throughout the Reich. 10. *Staffel* was credited with the *Herausschuss* of a single B-17 for the loss in combat of one Focke-Wulf, whose pilot parachuted to safety.

A somewhat smaller enemy force – nonetheless numbering close on 1,000 bombers – struck at aircraft plants and oil installations the following day. 10. and 11. *Staffeln* are reported to have put up just six Focke-Wulfs in opposition, the latter losing Unteroffizier Theodor Körner – shot down and killed over the Danish island of Lolland – in exchange for one more Fortress destroyed.

A third major effort in as many days by the Americans, which included a mixed force of over 700 B-17s and B-24s sent against airfields and other aviation targets within Germany's borders on 30 May, cost the attackers just 12 'heavies'. Again, it was 11. *Staffel* which was credited with the *Gruppe's* sole victory – another B-17 *Herausschuss*.

IV.(*Sturm*)/JG 3's unquestionably poor performance at the end of the month was in stark contrast to its earlier successes during the second week of May, when it had still been flying Bf 109s, and employing its tried-and-tested frontal attack tactics. Some sources claim that the *Gruppe's* remaining operational while carrying out its conversion to Focke-Wulfs was a mistake. This certainly contributed to the low numbers of machines being scrambled during the final days of May – some ten per cent, or less, of full establishment – and seems to bear out the views expressed by some of Hauptmann Moritz's pilots that an Fw 190-equipped *Gruppe* should have been selected for the *Sturm* role.

This may have been true in the short term, but in just over seven weeks' time IV.(*Sturm*)/JG 3 would be surpassing everybody's expectations and making national headlines as the Luftwaffe's foremost bomber-killer unit. But first its pilots were in for an even greater shock. In little more than a week's time they would be flying low-level *Jabo* (fighter-bomber) sorties!

JABO MISSIONS

The German High Command was aware that the Allies planned to mount an invasion of northwest Europe. What it did not know was the exact date and location. For some considerable time after the first troops had stormed ashore on the Normandy beaches on 6 June 1944, the Führer remained convinced that these landings west of the Seine were a feint. His refusal to allow local army commanders to bring in forces from the Pas de Calais and elsewhere to help repel the invaders was a serious mistake from which the defenders on the ground were never able to recover.

In the air there seem to have been no such qualms. The OKL had long had contingency plans in place to rush all available fighter forces into France as soon as an enemy landing was reported. These plans would be set in motion by the code message 'Dr Gustav West' (**Dr G**ustav **W**est indicated '**Dr**ohende **G**efahr **W**est', or 'Threatening Danger West'). Upon receipt of this message almost the entire strength of the daylight Defence of the Reich organisation (with the exception of four *Jagdgruppen* and a handful of *Zerstörer* and other small units) would move forward to take up station on pre-assigned airfields in France. JG 3's fields were concentrated to the west and southwest of Paris, which meant that it would be one of the *Jagdgeschwader* closest to the actual landing beaches.

When the coded transmission was received at Salzwedel on the morning of 6 June there was a burst of frenzied activity. An advance party of key ground personnel and their equipment were loaded aboard half-a-dozen Ju 52/3m transports which had flown in and were waiting to ferry them to Dreux – an airfield some 46 miles (75 km) almost due west of Paris. All six tri-motors arrived safely at their destination in the early evening of D-Day itself. Hauptmann Moritz and his three *Staffeln* departed Salzwedel for Dreux at 0700 hrs on 8 June, staging via Rheine and München-Gladbach (and, incidentally, leaving behind the attached 2./JG 51 to complete its reconversion to Fw 190s).

The *Sturmgruppe* touched down at Dreux shortly before 1430 hrs, and within minutes the air-raid warning had sounded. The bombs that followed caused no material damage. Over the course of the next five days the *Gruppe* would escape similarly unharmed from a succession of further raids on Dreux by both high-altitude 'heavies' and low-level fighter-bombers. The unit was either remarkably fortunate or extremely well dispersed!

The news that JG 3 was itself to be employed in the fighter-bomber role came as an unwelcome surprise, especially to the Fw 190 pilots of IV. *Gruppe*. It has been suggested that the choice of JG 3 for this task was dictated by the *Geschwader's* relative proximity to the landing beaches. But this was little comfort to Moritz's *Staffeln*, as the few mechanics available to them laboured to modify the machines' ventral ETC 501 racks so that they could carry 250 kg (551 lb) bombs in place of their usual drop tanks on their first *Jabo* mission, scheduled for the following morning.

The *Gruppe's* targets on 9 June were to be the invasion fleet off the Orne Estuary and enemy forces moving inland to the north of Caen. In fact, only 10. and 11. *Staffeln* would be carrying bombs, as 12./JG 3's Focke-

Armourers ready a 551-lb SC 250 bomb (which appears to be fitted with tailfin screamers) for attachment to a *Sturmbock* in preparation for a *Jabo* raid against the Normandy beachhead

Wulfs were unable to do so as they still had the *'Krebsgerät'* rearward-firing rocket tubes firmly attached to their bellies. Oberleutnant Hans Rachner's pilots were therefore ordered to provide fighter cover for the other two *Staffeln*. It would be hard to imagine a fighter less suited to escort duties than a heavily armoured *Sturmbock* encumbered with a ventral rocket tube. There was clearly something wrong somewhere.

In fact, there had been a breakdown in communications within the higher echelons of the OKL. All four *Gruppen* of JG 3 had indeed long been part of the anti-invasion contingency plans, but when they were all flying Bf 109s. Incredibly, it appears that somebody in the corridors of power in Berlin had failed to take note of the fact that IV./JG 3 had since converted to Fw 190s, and that now, as the Luftwaffe's only dedicated anti-bomber *Sturm* unit, it formed an integral part of the Defence of the Reich armoury and should never have been sent to France at all!

Meanwhile IV.(*Sturm*)/JG 3 was getting on with the war in Normandy to the best of its ability. Two *Jabo* missions were flown on 9 June without loss. Most pilots put this down to pure luck, but Hauptmann Moritz attributed it more to the judicious use of cloud cover. The *Gruppe* certainly led a charmed life, both on the ground and in the air, during its brief spell of operations on the western front.

During the next two days further fighter-bomber attacks were mounted against offshore shipping and Allied troops and armour north of Caen. Despite heavy anti-aircraft fire, and the enemy's overwhelming air superiority over the beachhead area, all the Focke-Wulfs again returned safely to Dreux. The pilots' total inexperience in dropping bombs meant, however, that there was little to show for their efforts – apart from at least one successful attack on a clutch of tanks which, unfortunately, happened to belong to the 12th SS Panzer Division *'Hitlerjugend'*!

Feldwebel Willi Maximowitz returns to Dreux with an empty bomb-rack after *a Jabo* sortie. Although wearing similar spiral markings, this is not the same machine as that seen in the photograph opposite – note the lack of 'blinkers'

Blinkered or not, forward visibility
from a Fw 190 when on the ground
was non-existent. Willi Maximowitz
peers cautiously out of the cockpit of
his 'Black 8' as a mechanic runs just
in front of the fighter, guiding the
pilot towards one of the field's
wooded dispersal areas

On 11 June the main body of groundcrew arrived at Dreux by road,
bringing with them the heavy equipment that would help ease the
workload of the overstretched advanced party. By now the *Gruppe's*
serviceability figures had sunk to less than half. But this was due almost
entirely to the lack of proper maintenance facilities. Records indicate that
only two Focke-Wulfs sustained slight damage (and this from accidental
causes) during the unit's time in France.

Other *Jagdgruppen* pressed into service as *Jabos* in Normandy had not been
so fortunate as IV.(*Sturm*)/JG 3. They had suffered appalling casualties.
The loss of experienced pilots for little or no gain led, on 13 June,
to the abandonment of any further such missions. It was only when the order
went out to cease these costly operations that it was belatedly realised that
IV.(*Sturm*)/JG 3 had been one of the units taking part in them.

As one story has it, it was *Reichsmarschall* Göring himself who, upon
being informed of the heavy losses being incurred by 'his' *Sturmgruppe*
while flying as fighter-bombers in the west, ordered their immediate recall
to Defence of the Reich duties. But this is almost certainly apocryphal.
Firstly, IV.(*Sturm*)/JG 3 had suffered no such losses – heavy or otherwise
– and, secondly, the Luftwaffe C-in-C had evinced little direct interest in
the *Gruppe's* activities to date.

Much more convincing is Hauptmann Moritz's recollection of Oberst
Hannes Trautloft's arriving at Dreux at around this time with instructions
that the *Gruppe* was to be transferred back to the Reich at once. Trautloft,
who was currently serving on *General der Jagdflieger* Galland's staff as
Inspector of Day Fighters West, went on to confide in Moritz that 'there
was an almighty uproar among the staffs as to who had been responsible
for sending them to the invasion front in the first place!'

Whoever the guilty party, the order was quickly rescinded. Turning
their backs on Normandy, IV.(*Sturm*)/JG 3 flew in to Eisenstadt, south of
Vienna, on 15 June. The feelings of those groundcrews who had only just
completed the perilous journey to Dreux and now had to retrace their steps
back halfway across Europe are perhaps best left to the imagination. For
Hauptmann Moritz and his pilots their finest hour was three weeks away.

OSCHERSLEBEN — NATIONAL HEROES

Even before the main ground party reached Eisenstadt, IV.(*Sturm*)/JG 3's Focke-Wulfs were on the move again. This time their destination was Ansbach, some 25 miles (40 km) southwest of Nuremberg. Arriving here on 21 June, and joined by 2./JG 51 – the latter now fully reconverted back on to Focke-Wulfs – the *Gruppe* resumed the training that had been interrupted by the foray into France.

This now consisted primarily of the three *Staffeln* perfecting their broad arrowhead approach flight formation, with 2./JG 51 flying cover in a similar, smaller arrowhead to the rear of, and slightly above, the main group. During this approach phase, the formation would follow the instructions of a ground-controller whose job it was to vector the *Gruppe* towards the enemy bomber stream. Once visual contact had been made, however, the leader in the air – usually Hauptmann Moritz – would order the arrowhead to split into its individual *Staffeln* (or even smaller units, such as *Schwärmen*, depending upon the size and composition of the enemy force to be attacked). Each one would then be assigned a specific box, or flight, of bombers as its target. If the Focke-Wulfs of 2./JG 51 were still in attendance and had not been drawn off into combat with enemy fighters, they too would be allocated a section of bombers to attack.

To achieve the maximum destructive effect, the order to fire would also be given by the unit leader. Officially, the *Sturm* pilots were supposed to be within 100 metres (110 yards) of the bombers before opening fire, but in practice the order to open up with the 20 mm cannon was usually given at a range of 400 metres, with the 30 mm outer wing MK 108s adding their extra punch at 200 metres. The latter weapons' ammunition magazines contained only 55 rounds per gun, which gave the pilot a fraction over five seconds of fire. It should be borne in mind, however, that just three rounds – literally a split-second burst – were usually enough to bring down a heavy bomber!

Upon moving to Ansbach, in southern Germany IV.(*Sturm*)/JG 3 had come under the control of 7. *Jagddivision*, headquartered in Munich. For operational purposes, the *Gruppe* was attached to Major Walther Dahl's JG 300.

This *Geschwader* had its origins in an experimental unit set up in June 1943 by ex-bomber pilot Major Hajo Herrmann, who contended that single-engined fighters could operate just as effectively by night as by day. Employed in the immediate vicinity of those areas under attack by RAF Bomber Command, where the night sky would be artificially illuminated by searchlights and flares, as well as by fires from the ground target below, the Luftwaffe's single-seaters (which were not equipped with radar) would be able to hunt the enemy bombers by purely visual means alone. This simple form of nightfighting, which was code-named *'Wilde Sau'* ('Wild

Putting Normandy behind him, Feldwebel Maximowitz next demonstrates a classic *Sturm* attack with these three gun-camera stills recording the demise of a Fortress . . .

Boar'), achieved some significant early successes. But it proved costly too, and gradually the unit's role changed, firstly from night to all-weather fighters and then, after some six months, to fully blown daylight defence fighters.

By the early summer of 1944, JG 300's three *Gruppen* – two of Bf 109s and one of Fw 190s – formed a cornerstone in the Defence of the Reich's order of battle. Indeed, it was the one complete *Jagdgeschwader* to be retained in Germany when all the others were despatched to the Normandy front. Major Dahl, the *Geschwader's* third Kommodore, had only just taken office. Prior to that he had spent two years as a member of JG 3, the last ten months of them as *Kommandeur* of III. *Gruppe*.

On 6 July 1944 Hauptmann Moritz and his men were ordered to move for the third time in as many weeks. A short hop north-westwards took them from Ansbach to Illesheim. Here they would also stay for just seven days, but they would be days long remembered.

The Eighth Air Force's Mission No 458 of 7 July was a major effort by all three bomb divisions, which despatched over 1100 B-17s and B-24s in total against strategic oil, ball-bearing and aviation industry targets throughout Germany.

. . . note the range from which the last frame was shot – just 90 metres, or 295 ft!

The much-decorated Major Walther Dahl, Kommodore of JG 300 – the *Geschwader* to which IV.(*Sturm*)/ JG 3 was attached upon its return from Normandy

At 0820 hrs on their first morning at Illesheim, 44 Fw 190s of IV.(*Sturm*)/JG 3 were scrambled to meet the attackers. At the same time Major Dahl and his three *Gruppen* of JG 300 lifted off from other nearby fields to the west of Nuremberg. Although the Moritz and Dahl formations were both ordered to fly northwards, they were on parallel but slightly divergent courses, and they never actually made contact with each other in the air.

Walther Dahl's mixed force of Bf 109s and Fw 190s was vectored towards several groups of 'heavies' in the Halberstadt-Quedlinburg area. In a sprawling series of engagements they claimed 29 bombers (27 B-24s and two B-17s) and six of their escorting fighters (four P-51s and two P-38s) between them.

Meanwhile, at least 20 miles (32 km) away to the north-northwest over the town of Oschersleben, Hauptmann Moritz's Focke-Wulfs had had the good fortune to encounter part of another bomber stream – a box of B-24s which, at that moment, was apparently devoid of all fighter cover. For the first time, and under near ideal conditions, IV.(*Sturm*)/JG 3's pilots were thus able to mount a concerted stern attack of the kind they had so assiduously practised over the past weeks.

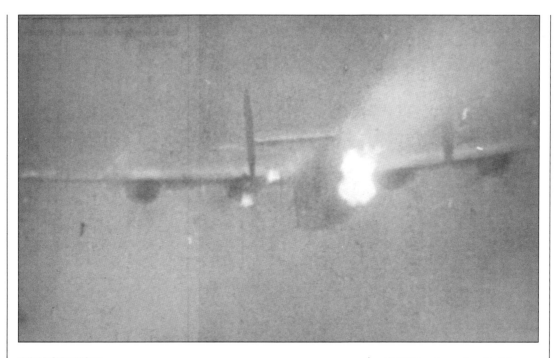

DEVASTATION

The effects of near simultaneous salvoes from more than eighty 30 mm cannon were devastating. As they barrelled through a sky of exploding, wildly spinning Liberators, the Fw 190 pilots were convinced that they had destroyed the entire box. With ammunition to spare, many of them went after a second formation of B-24s visible ahead of the first. In less than ten minutes the *Gruppe* had claimed a staggering 34 B-24s downed!

Among the victors, Hauptmann Moritz's single *Herausschuss* had boosted his total to 40. Werner Gerth of the original *Sturmstaffel* added two confirmed to his tally. The eastern front *Experten* of the attached 2./JG 51 contributed no fewer than 11 victories in this, their first Defence of the Reich action. A pair for *Staffelkapitän* Oberleutnant Horst Haase raised his overall score to 48, and a singleton for the *Staffel's* most successful pilot, Leutnant Oskar Romm, took his tally to 77.

Even 12./JG 3, incredibly still toting their under-fuselage rocket launchers, were credited with eight of the Liberators. Having been part of the massed attack from astern, 12. *Staffel's* pilots had had no opportunity to fire their rockets. The added weight of these missiles, whose very presence precluded the use of belly tanks, meant that 12./JG 3's fighters were much 'shorter legged' than those of the other *Staffeln* and, consequently, they had to look for suitable fields in the area where they could land and refuel, before returning to Illesheim.

Several opted for Bernburg, about 27 miles (44 km) to the southwest of the scene of the recent action. It was a fateful decision for *Staffelkapitän* Oberleutnant Hans Rachner, who was caught and shot down by P-51s just nine miles (14 km) short of his goal. The Mustangs also accounted for his wingman, Oberfähnrich Hans-Joachim Voss. Not that Bernburg provided much of a haven. The field had been one of the Eighth Air Force's objectives of the day, and 10. *Staffel's* Leutnant Alois Maier lost his

A B-24 Liberator under attack from astern takes hits on the tail and port inner engine

Leutnant Oskar Romm, wearing the Knight's Cross awarded on 29 February 1944 for his 76 eastern front victories

life while attempting to belly-land his damaged Fw 190 on its freshly cratered runway.

These were three of the day's five fatalities. The others were both members of 2./JG 51. Leutnant Werner Koch fell victim to return fire from the B-24s, while Unteroffizier Erich Nissler, who had put down briefly at Halberstadt en route back to Illesheim, was killed when his Fw 190 swung as he took off again. The only other casualty was Leutnant Hans Iffland of Hauptmann Moritz's *Gruppenstab*. Also hit by fire from the Liberators' gunners, the wounded Iffland baled out near Halberstadt.

As the after-action reports began to come in to 7. *Jagddivision* HQ, it quickly became apparent that the defending fighters had scored a signal victory. Over 80 claims had been made in all, but it was the *Sturmgruppe's* conviction that they had blown an entire enemy bomber formation out of the sky that grabbed the attention of the Luftwaffe brass and the imagination of the Reich's propaganda minister, Dr Josef Goebbels.

In the event, US sources would show that the 492nd BG – the unit first attacked by IV.(*Sturm*)/JG 3 – had lost 12 of its Liberators.

That same afternoon, even before Hauptmann Moritz had himself returned to base (he had landed at an airfield near Magdeburg as a precautionary measure to have makeshift repairs carried out on his damaged Focke-Wulf), both the divisional commander, Generalmajor Huth, and *General der Jagdflieger* Adolf Galland had flown in to Illesheim to get a first-hand account of the *Gruppe's* achievement.

To Galland's mind this was exactly the outcome predicted by Major von Kornatzki when he had first proposed the *Sturm* idea nine months earlier. However, the General did not lose sight of the fact that this one *Gruppe's* success, spectacular as it may have been, had not prevented the rest of the enemy bombers from getting through to their targets. To stop the Eighth Air Force in its tracks an even heavier blow was needed, and so, just as *Sturmstaffel* 1's initial successes had led to the creation of IV.(*Sturm*)/JG 3, the latter's present accomplishments were to be the trigger for the activation of further *Sturmgruppen*.

But time and the worsening war situation were not on the Luftwaffe's side. Just two further *Jagdgruppen* would see employment in the *Sturm* role. One, already flying Focke-Wulfs, would be converted and operational in five weeks, but the second, created from scratch, would not be combat ready until a month after that. In the meantime, with the Allies threatening to break out of their Normandy bridgehead and the Eighth Air Force preparing to resume its all-out daylight offensive against the Reich, IV.(*Sturm*)/JG 3 would continue to soldier on alone.

The publicity engendered by the *Gruppe's* success on 7 July would have even longer-lasting consequences – and of a very different kind. Eager for any item of genuinely good news by this stage of the war, the propaganda ministry in Berlin went into overdrive. Reports of the 'Blitzluftschlacht (Lightning air battle) of Oschersleben' appeared in newspapers and magazines throughout the land. Newsreel teams descended on Illesheim and footage of the *Gruppe's* Focke-Wulfs restaging the action were shown in cinemas nationwide.

Whether by accident or design, great emphasis was being placed on the part played by Major Walther Dahl, the *Geschwaderkommodore* of JG 300. The impression was given that he, personally, had led the

Sturmgruppe into the attack over Oschersleben. Below such headlines as 'Major Dahl and his *Sturmgruppe*' (admittedly, IV.(*Sturm*)/JG 3 *was* under attachment to his command at the time) there would follow accounts of the action written in the usual bombastic style of the day. A typical passage, for example, read;

'It is thanks in no small measure to the instinctive, tactical leadership of the Kommodore that this strong formation of fighter-bombers (sic) could be brought under attack. When the voice of the Kommodore suddenly rang out over the R/T, giving in short, concise words the order to launch the *Sturm* assault, then every last pilot in the formation was certain in the knowledge that this order had been given at exactly the right moment, and when he was in precisely the right position, to commence the attack.'

The propaganda bandwagon starts rolling. This article on the front page of Thursday 13 July 1944's *Hamburger Tageblatt* – Newspaper of the National-Socialist German Workers' Party – is headed, 'Major Dahl and his *Sturmgruppe* – Terror-formations destroyed to the last aircraft'

Even though he was known to be some miles away with the Halberstadt-Quedlinburg force at the time (where, according to his own after-action report, he had spent ten minutes trying to unblock his jammed guns!), Major Dahl made little or no effort to set the record straight. To be fair, once the propaganda machine was in full cry, it is doubtful whether he could have done so, even had he wanted to. But when he subsequently attempted to have IV.(*Sturm*)/JG 3 redesignated and officially incorporated into JG 300, it reportedly led to a distinct cooling of relations between the *Sturmgruppe* and their temporary *Geschwaderkommodore*.

Nor did Dahl's later book about those days in the Defence of the Reich help to clarify matters. Published in post-war Germany under the title *Rammjäger* (itself a misnomer), this patently self-serving work did not merely repeat the previous inaccuracies, it embroidered upon them. Now Dahl was portraying himself alongside Wilhelm Moritz leading the Oschersleben attack force;

"'Negus 1 to Caesar 1', I call to Hauptmann Moritz, "Do you see those two boxes in tight formation on the right flank? You take the left-hand one and I'll take the right!" Wingtip to wingtip, tucked in closely, we begin the second attack –

Another magazine – kept (and annotated) by a *Sturm* pilot for over 60 years – featured illustrations. Under the title 'Stormers of the Air', this photograph shows members of 10. *Staffel*, who were credited with eight of the 34 Oschersleben victories . . .

. . . and this is said to be one of the day's victims. Close scrutiny of the original cutting reveals it to be Liberator HP-Z of the 389th BG's 567th FS

This newsreel shot of a smiling Major Dahl (left) and Hauptmann Moritz appeared in newspapers and periodicals nationwide

the actual *Sturm* attack – from a shallow angle of 20 degrees below. Only some 600 metres (655 yards) now separate us from the bombers.

'The first stabs of fire erupt from the bombers' machine gun turrets. Our angle of approach is good. It can only be a matter of seconds before all hell breaks loose again. I give the order, "To all little brothers – close up tighter still for the *Sturm* attack! If you can't shoot one down, ram! Raaa-baza-nella!!"'

This total fabrication of events, ending with Dahl's own personal battle cry, together with the vastly inflated figures for enemy aircraft destroyed that are quoted in his book (greater even than the claims made at the time in the heat of battle), still rankled with some ex-members of IV.(*Sturm*)/JG 3 more than 40 years later!

Putting the apparent injustice of Oschersleben behind them, Hauptmann Moritz and his pilots transferred to Memmingen, some 62 miles (100 km) west-southwest of Munich, on 13 July. Here they were ideally placed to test their new-found muscle against the southern half of the USAAF's combined strategic daylight bomber offensive against the Reich – the aircraft of the Fifteenth Air Force flying up across the Alps from their bases in Italy. Within five days they would get their chance, and claim the greatest success of their entire operational career.

Behind the scenes, the expressions were a little more serious as Major Dahl makes a point to the assembled pilots of IV.(*Sturm*)/JG 3

In the left background of this frame – showing Dahl, Moritz and a group of officers including, second from left, 10. *Staffel's* Oberleutant Ekkehard Tichy – is a *Sturmbock* clearly bearing the number '13'

This photograpjh of the same aircraft, with another doing a victory pass overhead, was published in the Luftwaffe's own magazine *Der Adler* (The Eagle). Was Major Dahl photographed in the cockpit of this machine, as depicted by colour profile ten . . .

. . . or does this later shot of Major Dahl in another, 'unblinkered', aircraft show the real 'Blue 13'?

On 18 July 1944 over 500 B-17s and B-24s of the Fifteenth Air Force, together with their escorting fighters, lifted of from their Italian airfields to strike at aviation targets in southern Germany. Luftwaffe radar operators in the south were no less efficient than their northern counterparts, and the early-warning organisation quickly picked up the enemy formations and began monitoring their approach. After 30 minutes at cockpit readiness, IV.(*Sturm*)/JG 3 was ordered to scramble from Memmingen shortly before 0930 hrs.

B-17 BLITZ

For Hauptmann Moritz and his 40+ pilots, it was almost a rerun of the Oschersleben mission 11 days earlier. Vectored towards a strong force of B-17s coming in over Innsbruck, the *Gruppe* found itself on its own (Major Dahl's three *Gruppen*, plus one from JG 27 based in Austria, had been directed against other parts of the bomber stream which was now splitting up to attack individual targets). Turning in behind a sizeable formation of B-17s heading resolutely northwards, IV.(*Sturm*)/JG 3 was forced to break off its first approach due to the presence of large numbers of enemy fighters.

Then the *Gruppe* sighted a box of bombers which had become separated from the main body. The oft-practised arrowhead formation had suffered somewhat in avoiding the first box, and consequently the attack on the second was a rather disjointed affair. Nevertheless, as the heavily-armoured *Sturmböcke* knifed their way through, between and under the reeling Fortresses, it was clear that the Americans were being hit hard. Just how hard would become apparent when the post-action claims were assessed. In all, IV.(*Sturm*)/JG 3 would be credited with a staggering 37 enemy bombers destroyed, plus a dozen *Herausschüsse*.

In contrast to missions flown by standard *Jagdgruppen* when, if contact was made with the enemy, the lion's share of any resulting kills would

This still was taken from a propaganda company film shot on 15 July 1944 that purported to show IV.(*Sturm*)/JG 3 scrambling from Illesheim at the start of the Oschersleben mission. Close inspection of the machine on the ground (bottom left), with its breech cover hinged back, clearly reveals the absence of fuselage guns

When all the hubbub had died down, Major Dahl and Hauptmann Moritz found time to relax over a cup of coffee and discuss the mission

usually go to a handful of the unit's top-scoring *Experten* (and the crumbs to less experienced pilots), a *Sturm* attack – with everybody opening fire almost as one upon the given command, at close range and against a common, massed target – meant that victories were invariably spread evenly throughout the *Gruppe*.

Of the estimated 42 pilots who participated in the initial attack on the unescorted box of B-17s and then went on to engage other Fortresses in the vicinity, no fewer than 37 were credited with at least one victory. Ten scored doubles. The most successful of all, and the only pilot to achieve a treble, was Leutnant Oskar Romm, who had been appointed *Kapitän* of 12. *Staffel* after the death of Hans Rachner. This brought 'Ossi' Romm's overall score to 80. But the after-effects suffered by his having to bale out at high altitude meant that he would be off ops for the next two months.

Gruppenkommandeur Moritz's single B-17 took his total to 41. And one apiece for two of his *Staffelkapitäne*, Oberleutnants Hans Weik of 10./JG 3 and Horst Haase of the attached 2./JG 51, raised their tallies to 36 and 49 respectively. Leutnant Werner Gerth was one of those credited with a double, and many other familiar names from the original *Sturmstaffel* 1 – among them Oskar Bösch and Willi Maximowitz – featured among the claimants.

Coming hard on the heels of Oschersleben, this even more successful action to the southwest of Munich on 18 July did not command quite as much media attention. But this time credit was given where credit was due. Lumping together the aircraft destroyed with those claimed as *Herausschüsse*, the following day's High Command communiqué reported that;

'The Fourth *Gruppe* of *Jagdgeschwader* 3, under the command of Hauptmann Moritz, alone brought down 49 four-engined bombers.'

This was somewhat different from the communiqué that had been issued 24 hours after Oschersleben, and which stated;

'Fighting under the personal leadership of their *Geschwaderkommodore* Major Dahl, the IV. *Sturmgruppe Jagdgeschwader* 3, with their *Kommandeur* Hauptmann Moritz, particularly distinguished themselves by shooting down 30 four-engined bombers.'

A more tangible sign of recognition for Wilhelm Moritz's handling and leadership of the *Sturmgruppe* came in the form of the immediate award of the Knight's Cross, which was the first to be won by a serving *Sturm* pilot.

But 18 July had cost the *Gruppe* dear – six pilots killed in action, and a seventh so badly injured that he died the same day. Five of the fatalities had been tyros, shot down only minutes after claiming their first victories. Two had even been credited with doubles. Six other pilots had been wounded, including Hans Weik. Nor did the day's losses end there.

Once again, IV.(*Sturm*)/JG 3 had created undisputed havoc among a single bomber box. But, as at Oschersleben, the majority of the attacking force had got through to its assigned objectives. Unbeknown to Hauptmann Moritz and his pilots, their own base, Memmingen, had been this day's primary target for almost half the bombers despatched by the Fifteenth Air Force. Some 200 Fortresses, in four separate waves, plastered the field, causing severe damage and heavy loss of life. Among the latter were 12 members of the *Gruppe's* ground personnel. Of the nearly 60 aircraft destroyed or badly damaged on the ground (many of them twin-engined *Zerstörer*), eight of the unit's Fw 190s were complete write-offs and a further 13 would require major repair.

As a final postscript to this eventful day, it should be noted, perhaps, that the 483rd BG, which was the unescorted formation subjected to the *Sturm* attack, lost 14 of its Fortresses – a figure that was well under a third

After the euphoria of Oschersleben, reality soon set in again. And that reality came in the shapely form of the Mustang . . .

of IV.(*Sturm*)/JG 3's total claims. But such was the ferocity of the *Gruppe's* assault, and such the confusion reigning in that small patch of sky during those few indescribable minutes, that the bombers' gunners later estimated that they had been under attack from 200 fighters, and had shot down 66 of them!

In view of the devastation at Memmingen caused by the bombing raid, many of the *Gruppe's* pilots opted to land first at Holzkirchen before returning to base later in the day. Two missions in the next 48 hours netted the depleted *Gruppe* five and eight B-17s respectively. But each cost IV.(*Sturm*)/JG 3 two pilots killed. The mission of 20 July, against a deep penetration raid by the Eighth Air Force, had taken the *Gruppe* well to the east of its usual stamping grounds. Having to land away from base to refuel, the Fw 190s did not begin arriving back at Memmingen for several hours.

In the interim, the field had been subjected to another attack by Fifteenth Air Force B-17s, which cost the lives of 15 more of the *Gruppe's* ground staff. Hauptmann Moritz was immediately ordered to move the unit some 30 miles (48 km) northwards to Schwaighofen, near Ulm.

During the next eight days at Schwaighofen IV.(*Sturm*)/JG 3 saw little action. The time was taken up mainly in making good the recent losses suffered in pilots, groundcrews and machines. On 27 July 10. *Staffel*

To indicate their unique close-in role within the Defence of the Reich organisation, many of IV.(*Sturm*)/JG 3's pilots took to wearing 'Whites-of-the-Eyes' insignia on their leather flying jackets. This pair is modelled by 10. *Staffel's* Feldwebel Hans Schäfer, whose final tally of 27 kills included eight heavy bombers

celebrated the announcement of the *Gruppe's* second Knight's Cross, awarded to their recently wounded *Kapitän*, Oberleutnant Hans Weik, for his 36 kills to date. Two days later the *Sturmgruppe* was back in action when the Eighth Air Force again struck at oil industry objectives. The target for nearly 600 heavily escorted B-17s was the Leuna synthetic-oil plant near Merseburg. It was this force which Hauptmann Moritz and his men attacked (in the company of JG 300's two Bf 109 *Gruppen*).

Of the 13 US aircraft brought down in the resulting action near Leipzig, seven (six B-17s and a P-51) were credited to pilots of 2./JG 51. This *Staffel* also suffered the single loss of the day, but one of the Fortresses had provided *Kapitän* Oberleutnant Horst Haase with his half century. At least three of the remaining six victories went to ex-*Sturmstaffel* 1 veterans – Willi Maximowitz got a B-17, with Werner Gerth and Wolfgang Kosse claiming a P-51 each. With his score now standing at 24, Feldwebel Kosse was still working hard for his rehabilitation!

ACTION OVER HUNGARY

Twenty-four hours later it was the turn of the Fifteenth Air Force to target Axis oil. The pilots of IV.(*Sturm*)/JG 3 were sent up on their own against the bombers, which were reported to be heading for Hungary. They did not find the B-24s, which attacked the Lispe oil refinery complex without opposition. They did, however, sight a formation of B-17s whose objective was Budapest-Duna airfield. But the Focke-Wulfs were unable to penetrate the Fortresses' strong fighter screen. Instead, it was the aggressive P-38 pilots who broke up the *Sturm* assault.

In the ensuing free-for-all, the *Gruppe* was credited with a trio of Lightnings, all three downed in the area of Lake Balaton. In return, the P-38s claimed four of the *Sturmböcke*. IV.(*Sturm*)/JG 3's actual losses were two pilots severely injured – 2./JG 51's Leutnant Siegfried Schuster when attempting an emergency landing in his badly shot-up machine, and Feldwebel Willi Maximowitz, whose Focke-Wulf somersaulted on landing back at Munich-Neubiberg.

On 31 July the *Gruppe* transferred down to Schongau, close by the Austrian border. This put them right in the path of the Fifteenth Air Force's 'heavies', attacking targets in southwest Germany. But when the next such raid came in – a combined strike against industrial plants and marshalling yards in the Friedrichshafen-Innenstadt areas on 3 August – bad weather prevented Moritz's pilots from making an early interception.

Having scrambled from Schongau shortly after 1030 hrs, the *Gruppe*, escorted by the Bf 109s of I./JG 300, spent the best part of an hour searching for the enemy bombers. When they eventually found a box of some 30 B-24s (little more than 32 miles (51 km) from their point of take-off!), the Americans were already heading out across the Alps on their way back to base. A determined *Sturm* assault hacked down 19 of the Liberators in just six minutes (it is now believed that the 465th BG in fact lost 11 of their number to this attack). But these successes had not come cheaply. Nine Focke-Wulfs were shot down, with five pilots killed, one missing and one wounded. And the day's activities were not over yet.

In a telling demonstration of the weight and scope of the aerial assault now being waged against the increasingly beleaguered Reich, that same afternoon saw a force of almost 350 heavily escorted B-17s of the UK-based Eighth Air Force also despatched to strike at targets in southwest Germany. After the depredations of the morning, IV.(*Sturm*)/JG 3 could put up only six fighters to meet this new threat. One was shot down north of Strasbourg by return fire from the bombers, its pilot parachuting to safety. The other five were credited with the destruction of a Fortress each.

Never again would the *Gruppe* be able to claim two-dozen heavy bombers downed in a single day. During the remaining nine months of the war its pilots would top the 20-mark just three more times. Against this, their casualty rates would continue to climb steadily; and one of the blackest days in the unit's entire history was now less than a week away.

MUSTANG MAULING

The main weight of the Eighth Air Force's attacks of 9 August was directed against transportation targets in southern and southwestern Germany. Having recovered from its mauling of six days earlier, IV.(*Sturm*)/JG 3 put up a maximum effort in response. But on this occasion it was prevented from getting through to the bombers by the strong advance screen of US fighters flying ahead of the stream.

About 100 P-51s bounced the *Gruppe* from out of the sun as it flew in its usual broad arrowhead north-westwards across the Black Forest towards the oncoming Fortresses. There was no question of following the original *Sturm* edict that 'losses on the approach flight are to be compensated for by closing up on the leader'. The formation was scattered far and wide, and it was every man for himself. They were lucky to get away with just three pilots killed and one wounded.

Only two Focke-Wulfs managed to fight their way past the advanced screen and through the close escort to get at the bombers, where they claimed a B-17 apiece. Both were flown by experienced *Staffelkapitäne*. One was Oberleutnant Ekkehard Tichy, who had taken over 10./JG 3 after the wounding of Hans Weik three weeks earlier. Tichy had himself been severely injured back in March when, as *Kapitän* of 9./JG 3, the canopy of his Bf 109 had been shattered by return fire from the Fortress he was attacking and he had lost the sight of one eye. The other successful claimant was 11. *Staffel's* Leutnant Werner Gerth, who was also to be credited with a P-51 on this date.

The Mustangs had not finished with the *Gruppe* yet, however. Unnoticed, about 40 P-51s were tailing the *Sturmböcke*, which had reformed and were now heading back to Schongau. As they broke ranks to land, the USAAF fighters pounced. Seven more Fw 190s were shot down, with a further five pilots being killed and another two wounded.

9 August 1944 had, admittedly, been a particularly hard day for IV.(*Sturm*)/JG 3. But the ever-increasing strength of the opposition it was facing, the frequency and ferocity of the enemy's attacks and its own declining successes, coupled with the growing losses, was a situation that was being reflected throughout the entire Defence of the Reich organisation. The fears for the future once expressed by Major von Kornatzki were becoming a reality. The Americans had not been given a 'knockout blow', and the Luftwaffe's fighters were now in imminent danger of being overwhelmed by sheer weight of numbers.

The OKL sought desperately to remedy the situation. It had already pared other fronts to the bone to bolster the homeland's internal defences, so there was little further help to be had from that quarter. Furthermore, the USAAF's long-term offensive against the Reich's oil industry was beginning to make itself felt, although not yet among frontline units – the days of conserving every last drop of precious aviation spirit by harnessing ox teams to tow aircraft, rather than taxiing them about the field under their own power, were still some way off. However, at the training schools flying hours were being curtailed and courses shortened to keep up the flow of new pilots (despite the latter arriving in the frontline woefully ill-prepared) that were needed to make good the escalating rates of attrition.

One of the High Command's answers to this vicious circle was to increase the establishment of existing *Jagdgruppen* from three *Staffeln* to four. JG 3 underwent such reorganisation on 10 August. This meant that IV.(*Sturm*)/JG 3's three component *Staffeln*, hitherto numbered 10., 11. and 12., were redesignated and would henceforth operate as 13., 14. and 15. respectively. And the attached 2./JG 51, which had served for weeks past as a quasi-fourth *Staffel* within the *Gruppe*, was now officially taken on strength as 16.(*Sturm*)/JG 3.

It was in this new form, and in the company of the Luftwaffe's second *Sturmgruppe*, that Hauptmann Moritz's IV.(*Sturm*)/JG 3 flew its next mission five days later.

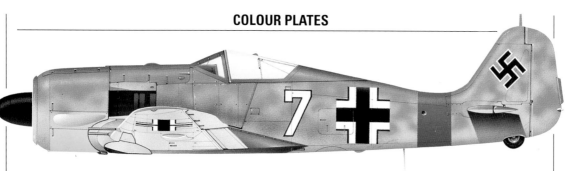

1
Fw 190A-6 'White 7' of Oberleutnant Ottmar Zehart, *Sturmstaffel* 1, Dortmund, January 1944

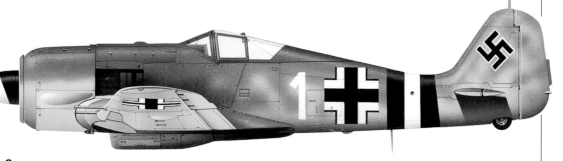

2
Fw 190A-6 'White 1' of Major Hans-Günter von Kornatzki, *Staffelkapitän Sturmstaffel* 1, Dortmund, January 1944

3
Fw 190A-6 'White 2' of Gefreiter Gerhard Vivroux, *Sturmstaffel* 1, Dortmund, February 1944

4
Fw 190A-7 'White 8' of Feldwebel Werner Peinemann, *Sturmstaffel* 1, Salzwedel, March 1944

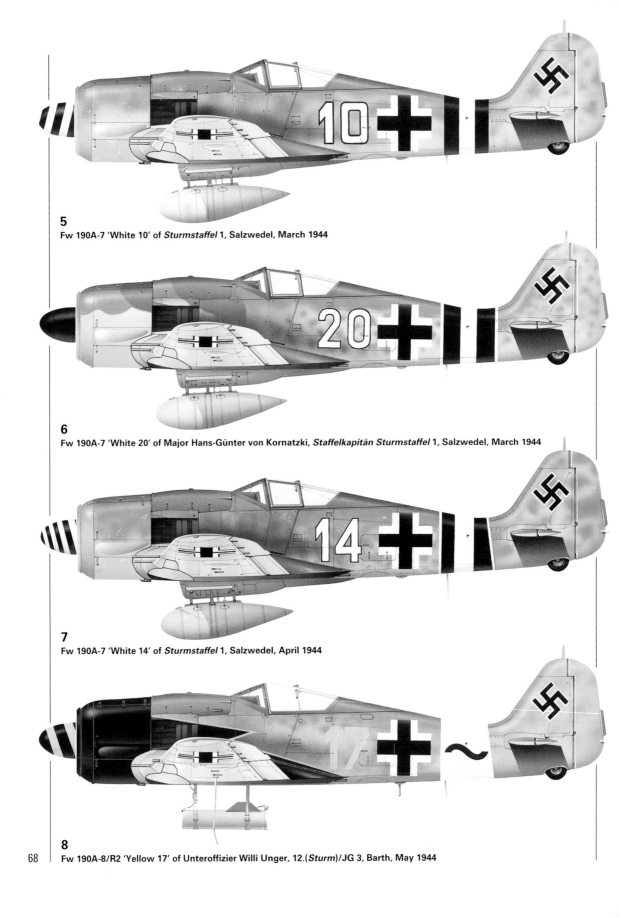

5
Fw 190A-7 'White 10' of *Sturmstaffel* 1, Salzwedel, March 1944

6
Fw 190A-7 'White 20' of Major Hans-Günter von Kornatzki, *Staffelkapitän Sturmstaffel* 1, Salzwedel, March 1944

7
Fw 190A-7 'White 14' of *Sturmstaffel* 1, Salzwedel, April 1944

8
Fw 190A-8/R2 'Yellow 17' of Unteroffizier Willi Unger, 12.(*Sturm*)/JG 3, Barth, May 1944

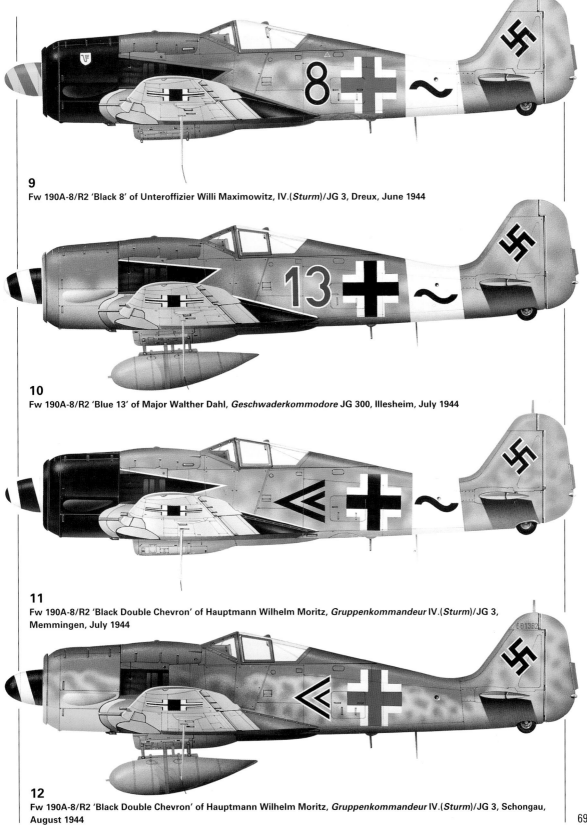

9
Fw 190A-8/R2 'Black 8' of Unteroffizier Willi Maximowitz, IV.(*Sturm*)/JG 3, Dreux, June 1944

10
Fw 190A-8/R2 'Blue 13' of Major Walther Dahl, *Geschwaderkommodore* JG 300, Illesheim, July 1944

11
Fw 190A-8/R2 'Black Double Chevron' of Hauptmann Wilhelm Moritz, *Gruppenkommandeur* IV.(*Sturm*)/JG 3, Memmingen, July 1944

12
Fw 190A-8/R2 'Black Double Chevron' of Hauptmann Wilhelm Moritz, *Gruppenkommandeur* IV.(*Sturm*)/JG 3, Schongau, August 1944

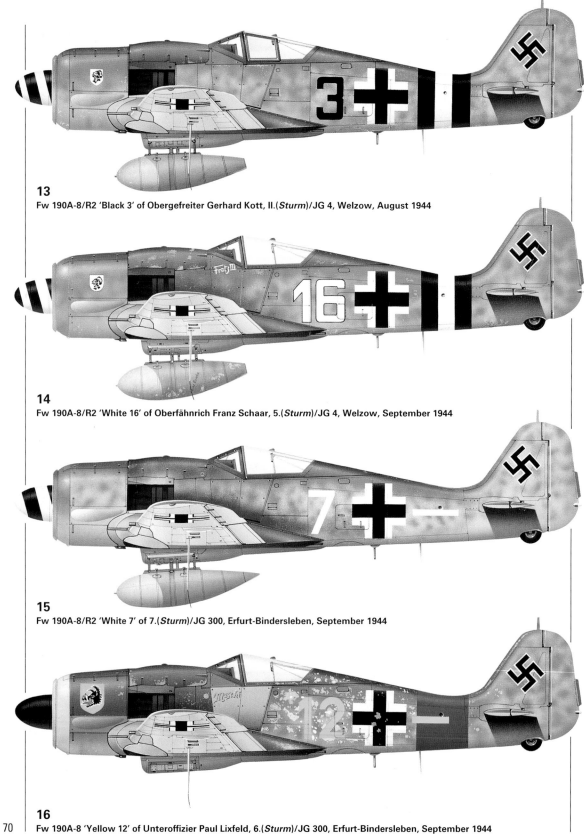

13
Fw 190A-8/R2 'Black 3' of Obergefreiter Gerhard Kott, II.(*Sturm*)/JG 4, Welzow, August 1944

14
Fw 190A-8/R2 'White 16' of Oberfähnrich Franz Schaar, 5.(*Sturm*)/JG 4, Welzow, September 1944

15
Fw 190A-8/R2 'White 7' of 7.(*Sturm*)/JG 300, Erfurt-Bindersleben, September 1944

16
Fw 190A-8 'Yellow 12' of Unteroffizier Paul Lixfeld, 6.(*Sturm*)/JG 300, Erfurt-Bindersleben, September 1944

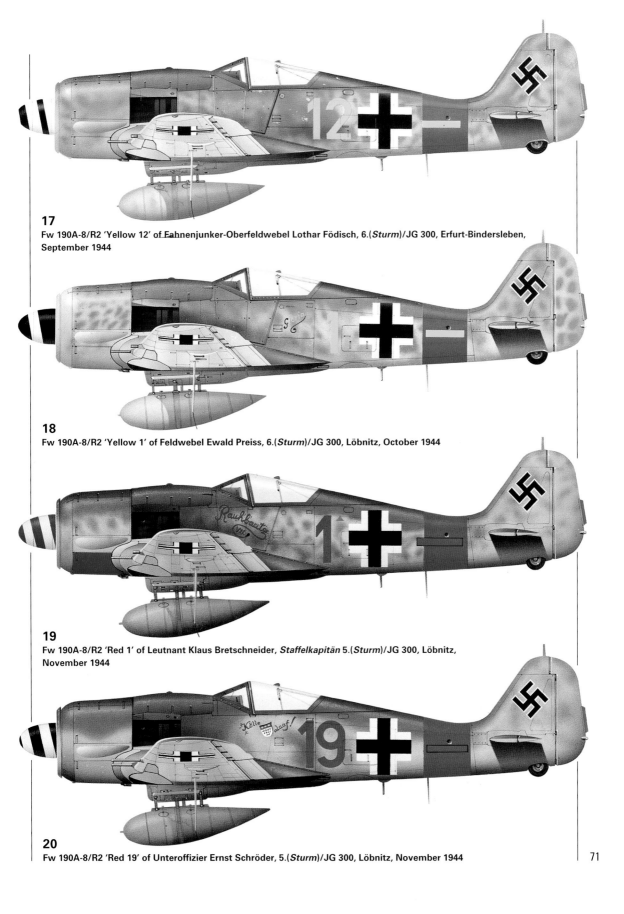

17
Fw 190A-8/R2 'Yellow 12' of Fahnenjunker-Oberfeldwebel Lothar Födisch, 6.(*Sturm*)/JG 300, Erfurt-Bindersleben,
September 1944

18
Fw 190A-8/R2 'Yellow 1' of Feldwebel Ewald Preiss, 6.(*Sturm*)/JG 300, Löbnitz, October 1944

19
Fw 190A-8/R2 'Red 1' of Leutnant Klaus Bretschneider, *Staffelkapitän* 5.(*Sturm*)/JG 300, Löbnitz,
November 1944

20
Fw 190A-8/R2 'Red 19' of Unteroffizier Ernst Schröder, 5.(*Sturm*)/JG 300, Löbnitz, November 1944

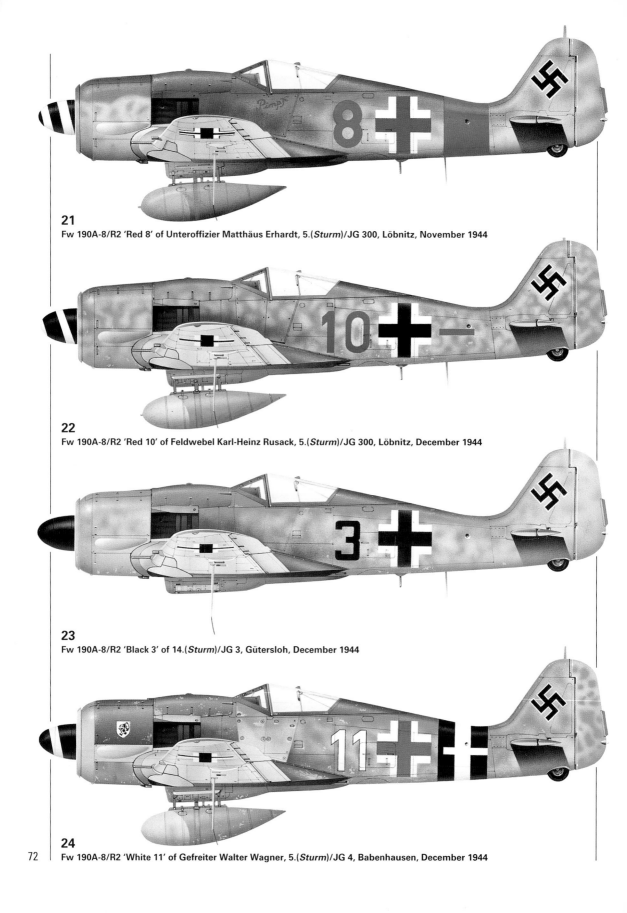

21
Fw 190A-8/R2 'Red 8' of Unteroffizier Matthäus Erhardt, 5.(*Sturm*)/JG 300, Löbnitz, November 1944

22
Fw 190A-8/R2 'Red 10' of Feldwebel Karl-Heinz Rusack, 5.(*Sturm*)/JG 300, Löbnitz, December 1944

23
Fw 190A-8/R2 'Black 3' of 14.(*Sturm*)/JG 3, Gütersloh, December 1944

24
Fw 190A-8/R2 'White 11' of Gefreiter Walter Wagner, 5.(*Sturm*)/JG 4, Babenhausen, December 1944

25
Fw 190A-8/R2 '00-L' of the 404th FG, Ninth Air Force, St Trond, January 1945

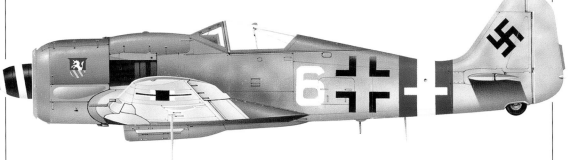

26
Fw 190A-8/R2 'White 6' of Leutnant Gustav Salffner, *Staffelkapitän* 7.(*Sturm*)/JG 300, Löbnitz, January 1945

27
Fw 190A-8 'Black 2' of 14.(*Sturm*)/JG 3, Prenzlau, February 1945

28
Fw 190A-8 'White 15' of Oberleutnant Anatol Rebane, II.(*Sturm*)/JG 4, Glücksburg, April 1945

1

Sturmstaffel 1
worn on cowling

2

IV.(*Sturm*)/JG 3
worn on cowling or below cockpit

3

II.(*Sturm*)/JG 4
worn on cowling

4

II.(*Sturm*)/JG 300
not worn on aircraft(?)

5

8.(*Sturm*)/JG 300
worn on cowling

6

7.(*Sturm*)/JG 300
personal emblem of Leutnant Gustav
Salffner

7

5.(*Sturm*)/JG 300
personal emblem of Leutnant Klaus
Bretschneider

8

5.(*Sturm*)/JG 300
personal emblem of Unteroffizier
Ernst Schröder

9

5.(*Sturm*)/JG 300
personal emblem of Unteroffizier
Matthäus Erhardt

PEAK STRENGTH, DIMINISHING RETURNS

I t was in the immediate aftermath of the Oschersleben battle that the Luftwaffe's second *Sturmgruppe* had been formed. Perhaps not surprisingly, the unit selected to undergo conversion was the Fw 190-equipped II. *Gruppe* of Major Walther Dahl's JG 300.

From its base at Unterschlauersbach, II./JG 300, then under the command of Major Alfred Lindenberger, had been the second most successful *Gruppe* in action on the day of Oschersleben. In the engagement over the Halberstadt-Quedlinburg area, it had been credited with 14 'heavies' and a pair of P-38s destroyed at the cost of three of its own pilots wounded. In the five-and-a-half weeks since that 7 July, II./JG 300 had been combining *Sturm* training with its operational commitments (in three days alone, 18-20 July, it had claimed 22 US bombers and ten fighters destroyed).

The Eighth Air Force's objectives on 15 August were Luftwaffe airfields in western Germany and the occupied Low Countries. The specific targets for the 200+ B-17s of the 1st Bomb Division were three fields at Cologne, Frankfurt and Wiesbaden. It was this force that the two *Sturmgruppen* were sent up to intercept.

At around 1000 hrs the Focke-Wulfs scrambled from Schongau and Holzkirchen (II.(*Sturm*)/JG 300 had transferred from Unterschlauersbach to the latter base on 13 July) and set off on the long haul north-westwards, escorted by the Bf 109s of I. and III./JG 300. It was a perfect summer's day, with hardly a cloud in the sky and almost unlimited visibility. Some 90 minutes later, just after crossing the Moselle valley, the fighters sighted the oncoming American formation in the far distance. Major Dahl who, as Kommodore of JG 300, was leading the *Gefechtsverband* (battle group)

From the same Fieseler manufacturing block as 'White 5' seen in the top photograph on page 76, Hauptmann Moritz's *Sturmbock* Wk-Nr. 681382 – complete with 'blinkers' – displays IV.(*Sturm*)/JG 3's new 'anonymous' finish minus the black cowling and white aft fuselage band at Schongau in August 1944

Above and below
These *Sturmböcke* of II.(*Sturm*)/JG 300 were photographed at Holzkirchen in late August 1944 at the start of their new career. The pilot snatching 40 winks in the shadow of 'White 5' (above) is Unteroffizier Friedrich Alten, who would go down in this machine (Wk-Nr. 681366) near Kassel on 11 September

ordered a wide turn to port to enable the two Fw 190 *Gruppen* to get into position for a stern attack.

Selecting a box of Fortresses temporarily devoid of its close escort of P-51s, the *Sturmböcke* bored in with all cannon blazing. Honours were almost exactly even – ten B-17s credited to the veteran IV.(*Sturm*)/JG 3 and nine to the tyros of II.(*Sturm*)/JG 300. In exchange for these 19 Fortresses (according to US sources this figure is more than double the number of bombers actually shot down, although it is still well below the astronomical 84 claimed by Dahl in his post-war *'Rammjäger'*, which includes seven shared among the six Fw 190s of his *Geschwaderstab* flight!) the *Gefechtsverband* lost six pilots killed and two wounded and twelve fighters destroyed. Most of the casualties were suffered by I./JG 300 in dogfights with the escorting P-51s.

After the action, Hauptmann Moritz's pilots were ordered to land at Frankfurt-Eschborn, where they would remain for the next few days as a precaution against further US raids on targets in the Rhine-Main regions.

The Fw 190s of II.(*Sturm*)/JG 300 landed where they could to refuel before the long flight back to Holzkirchen. One group of about a dozen, red fuel lights already beginning to wink, lobbed down in desperation on a small grass field just to the north of the Moselle, only to discover that it was being used solely for glider training. After a six-hour wait in the hot afternoon sun, a small amount of aviation fuel was trucked in – just enough for the Focke-Wulfs to make the short hop to a nearby fighter base, where they could refuel and re-arm properly.

Even with almost empty tanks and ammunition magazines, it would be a tight squeeze getting out of the pocket handkerchief-sized field. One pilot can still recall the heavy *Sturmböcke* ploughing through the metre-high grass before being yanked off at the very last moment, their wheels just missing the glider school's flight hut. All made it safely, eventually arriving back at Holzkirchen 11 hours after the morning scramble.

Creditable though the two *Sturmgruppens'* performance had been, it still fell far short of the 'decisive blow' for which they had been intended and which, it was hoped, they might yet deliver. But even if 19 enemy bombers *had* been brought down on 15 August, it was a casualty rate the now 'Mighty Eighth' could accept and absorb. It would certainly not discourage the Americans from continuing their ongoing daylight bombing campaign against the Reich's military and industrial strength.

The following day brought a decidedly less impressive result. Of more than 1,000 'heavies' despatched against oil and aviation targets throughout central Germany, just eight fell to *Sturm* assault. All but one were claimed by IV.(*Sturm*)/JG 3, which also suffered the sole fatality. Whether by accident or design, the one-eyed Oberleutnant Ekkehard Tichy collided with one of the 91st BG Fortresses under attack and both bomber and fighter went down. The *Staffel* that Tichy had commanded for less than a fortnight (the ex-10., now 13.(*Sturm*)/JG 3) passed into the capable hands of Leutnant Walter Hagenah. Tichy himself would be honoured with a posthumous Knight's Cross on 27 January 1945. Eleven of his 25 victories (including the last) had been four-engined bombers.

On 19 August the Fw 190s of IV.(*Sturm*)/JG 3 were ordered back from Frankfurt to Schongau. But they were soon on the move again. Forty-eight hours later they were sent to Götzendorf – a field just to the southeast of Vienna – in the expectation of renewed activity in that area by the Fifteenth Air Force.

'Black Double Chevron' kicks up dust (far right) as Hauptmann Moritz starts to roll. Note that 'Black 12' on the left still retains its black nose and 'lightning flash' paint job

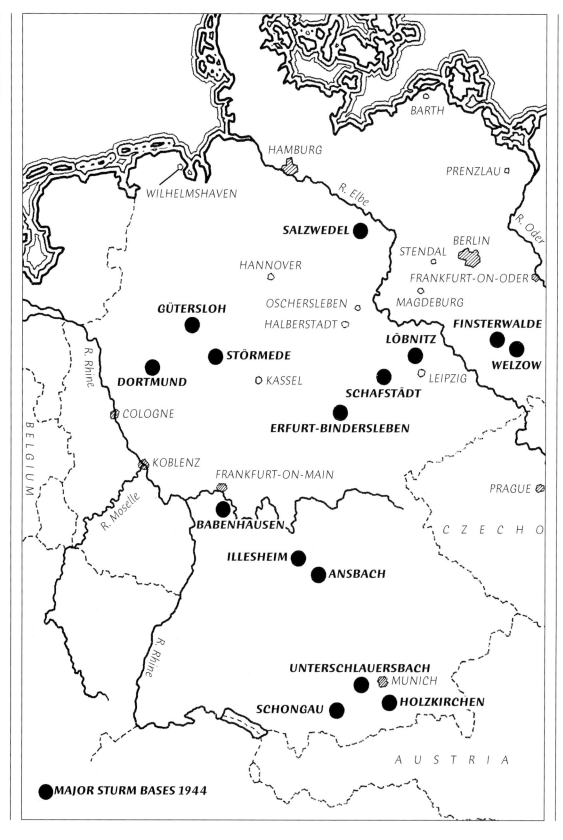

BARTH

HAMBURG

WILHELMSHAVEN

R. Elbe

PRENZLAU

SALZWEDEL

BERLIN

STENDAL

HANNOVER

FRANKFURT-ON-ODER

R. Oder

OSCHERSLEBEN

MAGDEBURG

GÜTERSLOH

HALBERSTADT

FINSTERWALDE

R. Rhine

STÖRMEDE

LÖBNITZ

WELZOW

DORTMUND

O KASSEL

LEIPZIG

SCHAFSTÄDT

@ COLOGNE

ERFURT-BINDERSLEBEN

B E L G I U M

@ KOBLENZ

R. Moselle

FRANKFURT-ON-MAIN

PRAGUE

C Z E C H O

BABENHAUSEN

ILLESHEIM

ANSBACH

R. Rhine

UNTERSCHLAUERSBACH

@ MUNICH

SCHONGAU

HOLZKIRCHEN

A U S T R I A

● **MAJOR STURM BASES 1944**

Luftwaffe intelligence was good. On 22 August a large force of B-24s did indeed lift off from their Italian bases to attack oil industry targets around the Austrian capital, including the underground storage facility in the Lobau district. With almost the entire Eighth Air Force anchored to the ground in the UK by bad weather, the Luftwaffe put up a maximum local effort – nine *Gruppen* in all – against this threat from the south.

Forming the spearhead of the defensive response, the two *Sturmgruppen*, accompanied on this occasion by I./JG 300 and I./JG 302, met the B-24s close to the Hungarian border some 80 miles (130 km) to the southeast of Vienna. In the attack that followed, 15 Liberators reportedly went down, with Hauptmann Moritz's 'Old Hares' again claiming just one more than the still relatively inexperienced pilots of II.(*Sturm*)/JG 300.

After hurriedly landing to refuel and re-arm, the *Sturm* units were sent back up to try to catch the bombers on their return flight. They failed to find the B-24s, but each *Gruppe* claimed a B-17 from another Fifteenth Air Force formation that was heading back through the same area. In addition, II.(*Sturm*)/JG 300 ended the day with four P-38s added to its scoreboard.

Good the Luftwaffe intelligence service may have been, but it obviously was not infallible. IV.(*Sturm*)/JG 3 had returned promptly to Schongau, only to be scrambled again shortly after 1000 hrs the following morning when strong enemy formations were again reported to be heading for the Vienna region. As the Focke-Wulfs set course eastwards, they were joined by II.(*Sturm*)/JG 300. But the only escort the two *Sturmgruppen* had was the half-dozen machines of Major Dahl's *Geschwaderstab* flight.

On 22 August the wounded Oberleutnant Hans Weik, walking with the aid of a stick and with his right arm still in a sling, visited his old 10. *Staffel* at Schongau to celebrate with them his recently awarded Knight's Cross. On Weik's immediate left may be seen Leutnant Walther Hagenah and Feldwebel Hans Schäfer

At Lobnitz a mechanic of 8.(*Sturm*)/JG 300 leans into the cockpit to make some final adjustments . . .

. . . before the pilot runs up the engine prior to take-off. On the right, *Staffelkapitän* Leutnant Spenst walks forward to deliver a few last-minute instructions of his own. Note that the unit is now sporting red Defence of the Reich bands

The mission completed – probably just an air test, as the drop tank is still *in situ* – the unknown pilot comes back in for a neat three-pointer

This time contact was made south-southwest of the Austrian capital. Hauptmann Moritz led his pilots in two separate assaults on an unescorted box of B-24s (machines of the 451st BG on their way to bomb Markersdof airfield). 'Emerging from cloud cover six to ten abreast and coming in with all cannons firing', in the words of one Liberator crewman, the Fw 190 pilots downed five B-24s on their first pass and added another four in the second attack three minutes later. One of the latter fell to Moritz himself. This ties in exactly with the nine losses suffered by the 451st BG, and proved to be one of the last big blows inflicted by Luftwaffe fighters on Fifteenth Air Force bombers during the closing months of the war.

In return, the B-24 gunners had claimed 29 of the Focke-Wulfs destroyed or damaged. Although this figure was a gross overestimate, the actual losses suffered by the *Gruppe* were bad enough – four pilots killed and a fifth missing.

Another 'black man' (Luftwaffe jargon for the ground mechanics in their dark working overalls) stands ready in front of his charge, awaiting the pilot's arrival

'Yellow 9' of 6.(*Sturm*)/JG 300 was used by Feldwebel Hannes Theiss to claim ten kills, including five four-engined bombers

6. *Staffel* pilot Feldwebel Ewald Preiss is pictured in the cockpit of his 'Yellow 1', which bears the name *Gloria*. Ewald Preiss would not survive the war, being one of the seven 6.(*Sturm*)/JG 300 losses suffered on 24 March 1945

IV.(*Sturm*)/JG 3 had been able to go after the bombers practically unhindered. This was due in no small part to the escorting P-51s concentrating their attentions almost entirely on II.(*Sturm*)/JG 300. The latter unit also sustained at least five known fatalities, but was credited with an equal number of Mustangs shot down.

The *Sturmgruppen* would be sent up against the Fifteenth Air Force on at least five more occasions before the month was out. On 24 August a mixed force of B-17s and B-24s attacked oil refineries in southern Germany and Czechoslovakia. The two *Gruppen* claimed five B-24s between them, but each suffered one pilot killed and one wounded. Twenty-four hours later, when the Fifteenth Air Force targeted airfields and aircraft factories in the Brno and Prostejov regions of Czechoslovakia, the *Sturmgruppen* failed to score a single kill, while losing five pilots.

Shortly after 0900 hrs on 29 August, about a dozen machines of IV.(*Sturm*)/JG 3 lifted off from Jüterbog, south of Berlin (where they had been on temporary detachment for the last two days), and set course south-eastwards for the Czech border, accompanied by the Bf 109s of III./JG 300. En route they were joined by the rest of Major Dahl's

Geschwader. After a good 90 minutes, and when over the foothills of the Carpathians, this *Gefechtsverband* sighted a heavily escorted formation of B-17s. The two *Sturmgruppen* pressed home their attacks. IV.(*Sturm*)/JG 3 claimed four of the bombers – believed to be from the 2nd BG – but lost a pilot, who went down over Trencin, Slovakia. II.(*Sturm*)/JG 300 also claimed four Fortresses, plus an additional pair of *Herausschüsse*, without loss.

To all intents and purposes this was the end of the *Sturm* campaign against the Fifteenth Air Force in southern and southeastern Europe. The *Sturmböcke* had inflicted some telling losses on the 'heavies' flying up from Italy, but that all-important 'decisive blow' still eluded them. The bombers of the Fifteenth Air Force, like their UK-based counterparts of the Eighth, were benefiting from ever stronger and more effective fighter protection. If the enemy's escorting fighters could break up the *Sturmgruppens'* carefully co-ordinated approach runs, then Major von Kornatzki's original concept of a concerted, mass attack would become increasingly difficult, if not impossible, to implement.

Nevertheless, the *Sturm* pilots, until overtaken by events on the ground, would continue to give of their best as they tried to carry out their own unique role in the daylight defence of the Reich. For the next three months their major battleground would be central and western Germany, and their main opponents the bombers and fighters of the Eighth Air Force. With their own numbers bolstered by the entry into service of a third (and final) *Sturmgruppe*, they would demonstrate that, when conditions were right, they were still a force to be reckoned with.

BASE MOVEMENTS

On 30 August IV.(*Sturm*)/JG 3 was ordered to vacate Schongau, in deepest Bavaria, for Schafstädt, an airfield some 110 miles (180 km) to the southwest of Berlin. It was at this time too that II.(*Sturm*)/JG 300 departed Holzkirchen for Erfurt-Bindersleben, half as far again from the German capital. For the two *Gruppen*, the first week or so at their new bases was to remain relatively quiet.

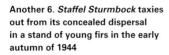

Another 6. *Staffel Sturmbock* **taxies out from its concealed dispersal in a stand of young firs in the early autumn of 1944**

Meanwhile, the long-awaited third *Sturmgruppe* was at last approaching the end of a protracted and costly period of working-up. This unit, II.(*Sturm*)/JG 4, was formed primarily around a cadre of pilots and groundcrews from a now defunct *Zerstörergruppe* that had previously been based on the French Atlantic coast. After converting from their twin-engined Junkers Ju 88s on to Fw 190s at Hohensalza, the ex-*Zerstörer* pilots moved to Salzwedel to join the new *Gruppe* – which had officially been brought into being on 12 July 1944 – to commence *Sturm* training.

They could not have wished for a better *Kommandeur* to oversee their transition than the 'Father of the *Sturm* Idea' himself, the now Oberstleutnant Hans-Günter von Kornatzki. Eager to see that his new command be given the best possible chance to put his 'massed stern assault' tactics into practice, von Kornatzki had also gathered around him a nucleus of original *Sturmstaffel* 1 pilots. Among them was Oberleutnant Ottmar Zehart, who had scored the very first *Sturm* victory of all, and he now became the *Kapitän* of 7.(*Sturm*)/JG 4.

After suffering at least two pilots killed and several injured during training, II.(*Sturm*)/JG 4 moved to Welzow on 31 August. Situated roughly the same distance to the southeast of Berlin as Schafstädt was to the southwest, Welzow was a large tree-girt landing ground quite capable of accommodating the *Gruppe's* full complement of 70+ *Sturmböcke*.

The three *Sturmgruppen* were now in place and awaiting the next major incursion by the Eighth Air Force.

It came on 11 September. Mission No 623 saw the despatch of over 1100 heavy bombers, escorted by more than 400 fighters, against a whole range of targets including eight synthetic-oil plants and refineries, an ordnance depot and engineering facilities. The Luftwaffe responded with practically all it had – more than a dozen *Jagdgruppen* totalling over 500 fighters. The *Sturm* units formed the defenders' main strike force, with two experienced *Gruppen*, their recent losses made good, plus a third (as yet unblooded, but at full strength and under expert leadership) thrown into action against the 'heavies'. Each had its own Bf 109 fighter escort. Had the day of the 'Big Blow' finally arrived?

The two westernmost *Gruppen*, IV.(*Sturm*)/JG 3 and II.(*Sturm*)/JG 300, took off first, both scrambling shortly after 1040 hrs. Led by Major Dahl's *Stabsschwarm*, and covered by I./JG 300 and I./JG 76, the formation was vectored south-westwards towards a large force of B-17s reported to be in the Eschwege area. Hardly had the enemy been sighted – some miles to the southeast over Eisenach – before the Focke-Wulfs of II.(*Sturm*)/JG 300, maintaining close formation and at an altitude of some 16,500 ft (5000 m), were pounced upon from above by a horde of higher-flying Mustangs.

The tight formation disintegrated into a violent free-for-all as the heavy *Sturmböcke*, all hopes of attacking the Fortresses dashed, sought to protect themselves from the lethal attentions of the Mustangs. It was hardly an equal contest. Although the survivors claimed an optimistic eight P-51s shot down, the *Gruppe* quickly lost ten pilots killed and two wounded.

Meanwhile, Major Dahl's *Stab* flight, together with IV.(*Sturm*)/JG 3, had managed to avoid the fray over Eisenach and were chasing back north-eastwards after another large group of Fortresses which had just bombed the Merseburg-Leuna synthetic-oil complex. They caught up

Right and below
Machines of II.(*Sturm*)/JG 300 are
lined up at readiness at Löbnitz in
September 1944. The parade-like
formation seems to suggest that
there is no fear of attack from
the air . . .

with the enemy 30 minutes later just short of Halle. Manoeuvring into position behind and slightly below one of the bomber boxes, the Focke-Wulf pilots adjusted their speed to that of the retiring B-17s. At a range of 220 yards (200 m) they opened fire, boring in to within feet of their selected targets before breaking off and diving away.

Sixteen Fortresses – most believed to have been from the 92nd BG – were reported to have gone down. Three fell to Major Dahl and his *Schwarm* and the remaining 13 were claimed by pilots of IV.(*Sturm*)/JG 3. But the latter were not to escape scot-free. The ubiquitous Mustangs were soon on the scene, and now it was the *Sturmböcke* who had to defend themselves. 14. *Staffel's* Leutnant Werner Gerth was credited with a single P-51 (which, together with one of the B-17s just downed, took his *Sturm* total to 25), but the *Gruppe* lost three pilots killed and two wounded.

And what of II.(*Sturm*)/JG 4? After more than an hour at cockpit readiness, some 50+ Focke-Wulfs were scrambled from Welzow. Rendezvousing with their III./JG 4 escorts over Finsterwalde, the *Gruppen* then spent a good two hours following ground control's directions, which gradually led them south-southwest until, shortly after midday, they finally sighted a mass of contrails close to the Czech border. These betrayed the presence of B-17s forming part of the 3rd Bomb Division force sent to attack refineries at Chemnitz, Rurhland and Brüx.

At 26,000 ft (8000 m) the pilots of II.(*Sturm*)/JG 4 curved in towards the bomber stream, most apparently aiming for the unprotected low formation of one of the trailing boxes. Despite their inexperience, they

. . . but once *in* the air, it was a different matter. Here, the end of yet another Fw 190 is captured by the gun-camera of a pursuing US fighter – and is that odd Y-shaped form near the bottom left corner of the film still the pilot making good his escape?

caused carnage among the Fortresses, being credited with 11 destroyed (a figure which tallies exactly with the losses suffered by the Ruhrland-bound 100th BG). But, as ever, the escorting P-51s were quick to react, protecting the B-17s from further assault and downing several Focke-Wulfs before the rest broke off in search of a less well-defended target. They found one in another formation of Fortresses heading for Brüx. Twelve more bombers were claimed, including one rammed by 8. *Staffel's* Leutnant Alfred Lausch, who lost his own life in the attack.

II.(*Sturm*)/JG 4's first operation had thus brought the unit 23 victories (seven of them *Herausschüsse*). But the price paid was heavy, with 12 pilots killed and four wounded. Twenty-three Focke-Wulfs had been lost – nearly half of those engaged!

The following day's press announcements spoke of an 'outstanding defensive success', with figures of 90 or more enemy bombers destroyed. Even the Americans admitted that it was the 'first major aerial clash experienced since 28 May'. But, in reality, 11 September was a costly setback for the Reich's Defence units. Some 113 fighters had been lost in combat against Mission No 623, and a total of 56 pilots had been reported killed or missing. The *Sturmgruppen*, despite all their efforts, had failed to deliver what was expected of them – not a single enemy bomber formation had been deflected from its assigned objective by their actions.

BOMBER DOMINANCE

As if to demonstrate their superiority, the American bombers – nearly 900 in all – returned to many of the same targets 24 hours later. The three *Sturmgruppen* were again among the defenders sent up to challenge them. Operating together as part of the same *Gefechtsverband* as usual,

IV.(*Sturm*)/JG 3 and II.(*Sturm*)/JG 300 were vectored to the north of Berlin, where they hit the B-17 bomber stream hard. In two separate attacks IV.(*Sturm*)/JG 3 was credited with seven Fortresses, but lost an equal number of Focke-Wulfs to the bombers and their escorting fighters, with three pilots being killed and two wounded.

On this occasion II.(*Sturm*)/JG 300 avoided the fighter screen long enough to get at the bombers as well, claiming a dozen of the B-17s. But it too lost three pilots, plus one wounded, in the day's engagements.

Meanwhile, II.(*Sturm*)/JG 4, accompanied by the Bf 109s of III./JG 4 and I./JG 76, had been directed westwards, where another formation of B-17s was reported to be heading towards Magdeburg. The Fw 190 pilots were unable to repeat their success of the previous day, but nonetheless claimed the destruction of eight Fortresses (one falling to the *Kommandeur* himself), together with five *Herausschüsse*. In return they lost eight aircraft, suffering four pilots killed and a fifth wounded.

One of the fatalities was Oberstleutnant Hans-Günter Kornatzki. His machine having been damaged during the attack on the bombers, the *Kommandeur* attempted a forced landing to the southwest of Magdeburg (ironically, not far from Oschersleben, the scene of the *Sturm* force's most publicised encounter with the enemy). Just before touchdown, however, von Kornatzki's 'Green 3' clipped some high-tension cables and cart-wheeled into the ground.

The loss of the 'Father of the *Sturm* Idea' was an undeniable psychological blow to all, and to none more than the members of his own fledgling *Gruppe*. II.(*Sturm*)/JG 4 had claimed the most *Sturm* victories in each of the two recent actions, but at a terrible cost in human and material terms. Nearly a third of its pilots had been killed or wounded, and over half of the 61 *Sturmböcke* that had flown into Welzow just 12 days earlier were now destroyed. This was a rate of attrition that no unit, let alone an inexperienced one, could be expected to bear.

Oberstleutnant von Kornatzki's place at the head of the *Gruppe* was assumed by Hauptmann Gerhard Schroeder, the *Kapitän* of 8. *Staffel*. But it would take some time to assimilate the many new pilots and replacement machines needed to bring II.(*Sturm*)/JG 4 back up to full operational readiness, and it was to be the end of the month before the unit flew its next *Sturm* mission.

As an interesting sidelight, while these newcomers to Welzow were being initiated into the procedures required for a successful *Sturm* assault, many of the survivors of the last two such attacks were intent on putting the experience behind them in time-honoured military fashion. So much so that the station commander at Erfurt-Bindersleben was forced to confine all personnel of II.(*Sturm*)/JG 300 to camp. One of the reasons given for this Draconian measure was the 'impossible behaviour' of the troops in local watering holes and other public establishments. Nor did the complaints of the surrounding civil population end there. It is said that when the *Gruppe* departed for Finsterwalde on 26 September, they left 20 pending paternity suits behind them!

The latter half of September had been a relatively uneventful period (at least in the air) for the other two *Sturmgruppen* as well. This was due mainly to a combination of bad weather and the Eighth Air Force diverting at least part of its energies to the support of the Anglo-American airborne landings along the river lines between Eindhoven and Arnhem in Holland (officially known as Operation *Market Garden*, but now much more widely known as the 'Bridge Too Far').

The operational lull did, however, allow both Walther Dahl and Wilhelm Moritz to be summoned (separately) to Hitler's 'Wolf's Lair' HQ in East Prussia to report personally to the Führer on the activities of the *Sturmgruppen* thus far and, presumably, to be asked their views on the road ahead in light of the recent loss of Oberstleutnant von Kornatzki.

Whatever decisions, if any, were arrived at, 27 September would, for the first time, see all three *Sturmgruppen* operating together in a single *Gefechtsverband*. The Eighth Air Force's objectives on that day included transportation networks and war plants in western Germany; and it was against the 2nd Bomb Division's B-24s, targeting the Henschel works in Kassel (producers of the much-feared Tiger tank), that the first massed *Sturm* assault would be directed.

IV.(*Sturm*)/JG 3 scrambled from its temporary base at Alteno at 1000 hrs. After rendezvousing with the other *Gruppen* (including I./JG 300, whose Bf 109s were to fly cover), the entire formation set course for Kassel. Some 45 minutes later contact was made with part of the attacking force to the southwest of the target area. The *Gefechtsverband* had chanced upon the 'wandering' 445th BG, which, having become separated from the main bomber stream, had opted for Göttingen as a target of opportunity and was now heading back out over Eisenach.

The three *Sturmgruppen* hit the unescorted Liberators in turn. The first to attack was IV.(*Sturm*)/JG 3. Flying their customary broad arrowhead with Hauptmann Moritz at the point, the pilots bored in close before splitting into *Staffeln*, their heavy 30 mm cannon cutting swathes through the hapless Liberator formation. In just three minutes they had claimed a staggering 17 B-24s destroyed, plus a further four *Herausschüsse*. Their own casualties amounted to just five pilots wounded.

Next to go in was II.(*Sturm*)/JG 300. The Liberator gunners were fighting for their lives. The *Gruppe's* 21 claims (a third of them

Aircraft of IV.(*Sturm*)/JG 3 taxi out at Alteno for the mission of 27 September 1944. All three *Sturmgruppen* were in action against an unescorted formation of B-24s on this date, with IV.(*Sturm*)/JG 3 being the first to attack. They claimed 21 Liberators . . .

. . . next to go in were II.(*Sturm*)/
JG 300, which was also credited with
21 B-24s. Two of the bombers fell to
Unteroffizier Ernst Schröder, seen
here on the wing of his famous *Kölle
alaaf!*. Lastly, . . .

Herausschüsse) cost it seven pilots killed, the sky now a tumult of burning
and exploding aircraft. One surviving B-24 pilot recalled the scene. 'At
one moment I saw four German fighters and five of our own bombers
going down around me. It was indescribable'.

One of the assailants, 5.(*Sturm*)/JG 300's Unteroffizier Ernst Schröder,
was more graphic in his description of the bloody clash high over Eisenach;

'As we approached in close formation we could see the results of the first
wave's attack – some bombers on fire, others blowing up. My *Staffelkapitän*
and I had a new type of experimental gyroscopic gun-sight fitted in our
fighters. This enabled me to claim two B-24s within seconds of each other.

'When I hit the first it immediately flipped over onto its side and went
down. Its neighbour was already damaged, the two left-hand engines
pouring smoke. The new sight allowed me to line up on him almost
instantly. Another short burst and he was enveloped in flames. I flew
alongside him for a moment, staring at the long banner of fire streaming
back beyond his tailplane. Then this great machine slowly turned over
onto its back before it too plunged earthwards.'

By this time a group of P-51s that had been escorting a formation of
1st Division B-17s near Cologne, some 100 miles (180 km) away to the

east, and had picked up the Liberators' calls for assistance when they first spotted the approaching mass of German fighters, were finally beginning to arrive on the scene – four minutes after IV.(*Sturm*)/JG 3's first unopposed pass.

Despite their belated appearance, the Mustangs may have been responsible for some of II.(*Sturm*)/JG 300's losses. They certainly inflicted heavy casualties on the reconstituted II.(*Sturm*)/JG 4, whose pilots were in the last of the three waves to go in. The *Gruppe's* subsequent claims for 25 B-24s destroyed, plus a further 14 *Herausschüsse*, are patently wide of the mark (the bomber formation was never that large to start with, let alone after the first two attacks!), but the inexperience of many of the pilots in this, their baptism of fire, should perhaps be taken into account.

There are fewer uncertainties about the unit's casualties. At least 13 of its *Sturmböcke* were hit, and seven pilots were reported killed or missing, with another three wounded. Nor were the losses restricted to the ranks of the replacements, for among the missing was arguably one of the most experienced *Sturmpiloten* of all – the veteran *Staffelkapitän* of 7.(*Sturm*)/JG 4, Oberleutnant Ottmar Zehart. His wingman that day was Obergefreiter Gerhard Kott, who recalled;

'After our first pass we wanted to re-form for a second attack. But hardly had the *Gruppe* got itself into some sort of formation before I saw Zehart's machine rapidly losing height. He was later posted as missing.'

And Ottmar Zehart, whose 'Yellow 2' went down somewhere near Brunswick, remains missing to this day.

. . . it was the turn of II.(*Sturm*)/JG 4. Its pilots claimed the destruction of a staggering 39(!) Liberators. The five NCO pilots of 5. *Staffel* pictured here, from left to right, are Unteroffiziere Barion and Chlond, Feldwebel Berg and Unteroffiziere Keller and Erler. They accounted for nine bombers between them

II.(*Sturm*)/JG 4's haul of Liberators cost it seven pilots killed or missing. Obergefreiter Gerhard Kott, pictured here, was flying wingman to Oberleutnant Ottmar Zehart, and witnessed the *Kapitän* of 7. *Staffel* go down

The *Sturmgruppen's* claims for a total of 81 Liberators (plus six Mustangs) are, of course, exaggerated. But there is no denying the fact that they had inflicted grievous wounds upon the 445th BG. With 26 of its 37 B-24s failing to return, this represented the largest loss by any single USAAF group on any single mission during the entire war.

But not even a massacre on this scale could halt the juggernaut that the Eighth Air Force had by now become. Twenty-four hours later the 2nd Bomb Division sent its Liberators back to Henschel's Kassel plant. This time, however, the *Sturmgruppen* were engaged elsewhere – against the B-17s of the 1st Bomb Division, targeting Magdeburg.

In a rerun of the previous day's action, all three *Gruppen* concentrated in turn on a single box – the Fortresses of the 303rd BG (see *Osprey Aviation Elite Units 11 – 303rd Bombardment Group* for further details). II.(*Sturm*)/JG 4 went in first, followed by IV.(*Sturm*)/JG 3 and with the *Stabsschwarm* and II.(*Sturm*)/JG 300 bringing up the rear. The results were more modest, with 29 B-17s being claimed (the 303rd actually lost 11) before the *Sturmböcke* were set upon by US fighters. In the course of individual dogfights spreading over a wide area, the heavy Fw 190s claimed a single P-51 and a pair of P-38s (the latter not substantiated by post-war records).

Gerhard Kott was another of 27 September's claimants. On 14 October he received the Iron Cross, 1st Class, for a total of five four-engined bombers shot down (the first while serving with IV.(*Sturm*)/JG 3. The award certificate, signed by Generaloberst Stumpff, GOC Luftflotte Reich, is reproduced here

IM NAMEN DES FÜHRERS UND OBERSTEN BEFEHLSHABERS DER WEHRMACHT

VERLEIHE ICH
DEM

Unteroffizier
Gerhard K o t t
6.(Sturm)/J.G. 4

DAS

EISERNE KREUZ 1. KLASSE

H.Qu. .... den 14.Okt. 19 44
Der Oberbefehlshaber der Luftflotte Reich

Generaloberst
(DIENSTGRAD UND DIENSTSTELLUNG)

COSTLY LOSSES

The loss of 12 aircraft, while representing well over 100 personal tragedies, was something the 'Mighty Eighth' could take in its stride. But the 17 pilots and 22 machines lost to the *Sturmgruppen* on this 28 September was yet more bloodletting they could ill afford. The brief employment of a 'Big Wing' of all three *Sturmgruppen* operating together had not proved a success. Utilising their combined resources to maul one box of bombers, however savagely, was not going to prevent the rest of the huge enemy streams from continuing on to their assigned objectives. In the process, the Luftwaffe defenders were inevitably losing the war of attrition. A change of plan was called for, and with it came the beginning of the end for the *Sturmgruppen* as specialised bomber-killer units.

On 29 September Major Heinz Bär, then the *Geschwaderkommodore* of JG 3, visited Moritz and his men at their temporary Alteno base. Unlike IV.(*Sturm*)/JG 3, Bär's other three *Gruppen* had been retained in Normandy and on the western front. They had all suffered heavily in the retreat from France, and had only recently been withdrawn to the Reich for rest and re-equipment. Now, Bär informed Moritz, the *Sturmgruppe* was to be returned to the control of its parent *Geschwader*.

5. *Staffel's* Oberfähnrich Franz Schaar – pictured here perched on the cockpit sill of his *Fratz III*, victory stick in hand – was one of II.(*Sturm*)/JG 4's three wounded of 27 September

Sturmstaffel 1 veteran Leutnant Walter Peinemann was one of 17 *Sturm* pilots killed on 28 September 1944, although unlike the vast majority of his comrades to die on this date, he did not fall in combat. Instead, he was killed in an accident whilst attempting to take off from Welzow in an Fw 190A-8/R2 from 7.(*Sturm*)/JG 4

A few days later IV.(*Sturm*)/JG 3 flew back to Schafstädt, thereby ending its long association with Major Walther Dahl's JG 300.

The *Gruppe's* first mission on its own could hardly be termed successful. On 6 October the Eighth Air Force's B-17s mounted a twin-pronged attack on mainly industrial targets and military installations in northern Germany. Scrambling from Schafstädt shortly before noon, the Fw 190s of IV.(*Sturm*)/JG 3 were directed northwards against the 400+ Fortresses of the 1st Bomb Division heading for towns and airfields in the Baltic coastal region. Before they could reach the bomber stream, however, they were intercepted by Mustangs south of Stettin. Two *Sturmböcke* were shot down, their pilots killed and many more aircraft damaged.

The rest of the *Gruppe* scattered, with a number of pilots subsequently putting down at Alteno due to a lack of fuel. Here, at least two more Focke-Wulfs were written-off in landing accidents. One pilot lost his life, while the other, already severely wounded in the clash with the P-51s, sustained further injuries. This was Feldwebel Gerhard Vivroux, formerly

11.(*Sturm*)/JG 3's Unteroffizier Gerhard Vivroux is seen here wearing a flying jacket adorned with the distinctive 'Whites-of-the-Eyes' emblem that was unique to the *Jagdwaffe's Sturm* pilots. One of the most successful members of *Sturmstaffel* 1 with five kills to his credit, Vivroux had increased his tally to 11 by the time he was severely wounded in action during a clash with P-51s on 6 October. Suffering further injuries when he crashed landed his damaged fighter at Alteno, Vivroux finally succumbed to his wounds 19 days later of *Sturmstaffel* 1, and one of the *Gruppe's* most experienced members. He died in hospital just under three weeks later.

While IV.(*Sturm*)/JG 3 had been engaged up near the Baltic, the main weight of the Luftwaffe's defensive response had been thrown against the B-17s of the 3rd Bomb Division attacking targets in the greater Berlin area. Among the units sent up to defend the capital was II.(*Sturm*)/JG 4.

After taking off from Welzow, the Fw 190s of the *Sturmgruppe* met up with III./JG 4's Bf 109s over Finsterwalde, and together the two *Gruppen* set course north-westwards. They sighted the approaching enemy bomber stream between Brandenburg and Potsdam. Making a wide turn to get in behind the B-17s, they hit the Fortresses while they were still some 31 miles (50 km) short of their objective.

Even taking into account their recent propensity for overestimation, the *Sturmgruppe's* claims for 22 Fortresses downed (seven of them *Herausschüsse*) marked another significant victory. But it was to be the last such major success for the *Gruppe's* short-lived operational career as a true *Sturm* unit. And it had not come cheaply. Seven pilots had been killed and a further three wounded. Among the former was another of the original *Sturmstaffel* 1 veterans, Leutnant Rudolf Metz, whose 'Green 2' went down north of Brandenburg.

Little is known of II.(*Sturm*)/JG 300's activities in the Berlin area on this 6 October, but it was back in the thick of things 24 hours later when the Eighth Air Force struck yet again at the Reich's already sorely battered oil refineries. Among the eight Fortresses credited to the *Gruppe* near Merseburg was a unique treble for Leutnant Klaus Bretschneider, *Staffelkapitän* of 5.(*Sturm*)/JG 300, who brought down two B-17s with cannon fire and then added a third by ramming!

The other two *Sturmgruppen* were also aloft on 7 October as part of the Luftwaffe's concerted attempt to protect what little remained of Germany's

Two markings oddities carried by *Sturmböcke* of II.(*Sturm*)/JG 300, circa autumn 1944, but harking back to the *Gruppe's* days as a *'Wilde Sau'* nightfighter unit. Unteroffizier Paul Lixfeld of 6. *Staffel* poses in front of his very battered-looking 'Yellow 12', which clearly sports a rather large representation of the original boar's head emblem of the *'Wilde Sau'* units . . .

. . . while 8. *Staffel's* crest, although featuring a spear-wielding (but altogether friendlier looking) boar trotting over a map of Europe, still provides him with a lantern to light the way

vital oil industry. IV.(*Sturm*)/JG 3 matched II.(*Sturm*)/JG 300's claims for eight B-17s destroyed, and managed to do so without loss (two of JG 300's *Sturm* pilots had been killed). II.(*Sturm*)/JG 4 also suffered two fatalities, plus one wounded, in exchange for the seven Fortresses its pilots downed.

After the 23 B-17s (and single P-51) claimed on 7 October, the rest of the month was fairly quiet as far as the three *Sturmgruppen* were concerned. Although the Eighth Air Force kept up its attack on targets throughout the Reich, the 'heavies' were not subjected to *Sturm* assault. This was partly due to the increasingly parlous fuel situation, but also to the need for the three *Gruppen* to make good their recent losses in men and machines. One of JG 4's *Sturmstaffeln*, for example, had by now been reduced to just four pilots, while II.(*Sturm*)/JG 300's overall losses since June totalled 73 killed, two missing and 32 wounded!

All basic *Sturm* training was now being undertaken by a single *Schulstaffel* based at Liegnitz. But the replacement pilots were still far from combat ready when they arrived at their respective *Gruppen*, and a lot more practical instruction – or, at least, as much as the fuel supplies would allow – was required if they were to survive their first operational mission.

Fuel was scarce and pilot training barely adequate. The only thing there was no shortage of was aircraft. Despite all the Eighth Air Force's efforts to bring Germany's aviation industry to its knees, fighter production was to reach its all-time peak in the autumn of 1944. In the month of October, IV.(*Sturm*)/JG 3 alone took delivery of no fewer than 56 replacement Fw 190s.

The main reason for the building up and conserving of forces, however, was the plan currently being formulated by *General der Jagdflieger* Adolf Galland for the ultimate 'Big Blow'. This the *Sturm* units had so far failed to deliver. Now Galland planned to take the concept one

stage further by using the entire fighter strength employed on Defence of the Reich duties in one massive, co-ordinated strike against the Eighth Air Force. If this could decimate a complete bomber stream, then the tables might yet be turned in the daylight battle for Germany's skies – at the very least, it might gain sufficient time for the revolutionary new Messerschmitt Me 262 jet fighter (see *Osprey Aircraft of the Aces 17 – German Jet Aces of World War 2* for further details) to be put into frontline service in significant numbers.

But the *General der Jagdflieger's* strategy would never be put to the test. It was to founder on the twin rocks of interference from above and the demands of the war on the ground.

BRIEF RESPITE

Oblivious to this high-level planning, the three *Sturmgruppen* were content simply to enjoy their three weeks' respite. After an abortive attempt by IV.(*Sturm*)/JG 3 to intercept an incursion by Fifteenth Air Force 'heavies' against targets in Austria and Czechoslovakia on 16 October, during which 15. *Staffel* lost a pilot to P-51s, the latter half of the month remained closed in by predominantly bad weather.

It was during this period that four *Sturm* pilots – two each from IV.(*Sturm*)/JG 3 and II.(*Sturm*)/JG 300 – were awarded the Knight's Cross. The first to be recognised, on 23 October, was 15.(*Sturm*)/JG 3's Fahnenjunker-Feldwebel Willi Unger, whose total was currently standing at 20, all of them four-engined bombers.

On 29 October two awards were made, one going to Oberleutnant Werner Gerth, who had so often led the original *Sturmstaffel* 1 in combat before being appointed as *Kapitän* of 11. (the later 14.) (*Sturm*)/JG 3. His number of *Sturm* victories had by this time risen to 26. The day's second

Another 'Yellow 12' of 6.(*Sturm*)/ JG 300 was that flown by Fahnenjunker-Oberfeldwebel Lothar Födisch. After Födisch lost his life in another machine on 7 October, this particular aircraft became 7. *Staffel's* 'Blue 15'

Oberfeldwebel Konrad 'Pitt' Bauer wears the Knight's Cross awarded to him on 31 October. By war's end, Oberleutnant Bauer was serving as *Kapitän* of 5.(*Sturm*)/JG 300 and, with a score of 68 (including 32 'heavies'), had been nominated for the Oak Leaves

recipient was Major Kurd Peters, an ex-reconnaissance pilot who had taken over command of II.(*Sturm*)/JG 300 late in July. With no known victories to his credit, it must be assumed that he received the decoration for his qualities of leadership.

The last of the quartet, honoured on 31 October, was Feldwebel Konrad Bauer. Joining II.(*Sturm*)/JG 300 in June 1944 after serving with JG 51 on the eastern front, where he had scored his first 18 kills, 'Pitt' Bauer had since increased his overall total to 34.

A fifth Knight's Cross, awarded on 24 October, had gone to Hauptmann Horst Haase, the *Kapitän* of 2./JG 51 – the *Staffel* which had long been attached to IV.(*Sturm*)/JG 3, before being officially incorporated into the *Gruppe* as its new 16. *Staffel* on 10 August. Horst Haase had added ten *Sturm* kills to his previous eastern front tally of 46 prior to his transfer to the command of I./JG 3 on 3 October.

On 2 November the relatively tranquil existence of at least two of the Luftwaffe's *Sturmgruppen* was shattered by the Eighth Air Force's returning in force to strike yet again at the Reich's oil-producing plants. Close on a thousand 'heavies' were despatched against synthetic-oil

This portrait of IV.(*Sturm*)/JG 3's Feldwebel Klaus Neumann shows him as an archetypal *Sturm Experte*, sporting both the Knight's Cross (won on 9 December) and the 'Whites-of-the Eyes' insignia. The last five of Neumann's 37 victories (of which 19 were four-engined bombers) were achieved while flying the Me 262

Awarded a Knight's Cross on 29 October 1944 following 26 *Sturm* victories with *Sturmstaffel* 1 and 11. and 14.(*Sturm*)/JG 3, Leutnant Werner Gerth claimed his 27th success on 2 November when he rammed a B-17 north of Bitterfeld. Although the ace managed to bale out successfully, his parachute failed to open and he fell to his death

installations in central Germany, the main target being the huge Leuna complex outside Merseburg.

Scrambling from Schafstädt shortly after 1130 hrs, IV.(*Sturm*)/JG 3 first met up with the Bf 109s of I. and II./JG 3 before setting course almost due east towards the last reported position of the main bomber stream. They sighted the enemy some 30 minutes later to the northwest of Leipzig. While the Bf 109s fought desperately to keep the strong force of escorting P-51s off their backs, the *Sturmböcke*, led as usual by the now Major Wilhelm Moritz, bored in to the attack.

In the ensuing mayhem the *Gruppe* downed 21 Fortresses. One was claimed by the *Gruppenkommandeur* himself (his 44th victory), while no fewer than five of his pilots were credited with doubles. Among the latter was *Sturmstaffel* 1 veteran Feldwebel Willi Maximowitz, by now long recovered from his July injuries. Another was Feldwebel Klaus Neumann, ex-2./JG 51, whose brace of B-17s on this day took his score to 32, for which he would receive the Knight's Cross on 9 December.

But, as so often in the past, success had come at a heavy price. IV.(*Sturm*)/JG 3 also lost exactly 21 of its own machines, with ten pilots

99

This photograph of Leutnant Klaus Bretschneider, *Kapitän* of 5.(*Sturm*)/JG 300, was taken upon the occasion of his winning the Knight's Cross on 18 November. Less than a month later, on Christmas Eve 1944, he would be lost in action against USAAF Mustangs

Two of Bretschneider's 5. *Staffel* pilots, Unteroffiziere Matthäus Erhardt (left) and Ernst Schröder, pose in front of the former's 'Red 8', named *Pimpf*

being reported killed or missing, plus another five wounded. Among the dead was the Knight's Cross holder of just four days, Oberleutnant Werner Gerth. The *Kapitän* of 14. *Staffel* had claimed his 27th, and final, victory by ramming. Whether this act was deliberate or not remains unknown, for although Werner Gerth managed to extricate himself from his damaged fighter before it went down north of Leipzig, his parachute failed to open.

II.(*Sturm*)/JG 4 had lifted off from Welzow some ten minutes after IV.(*Sturm*)/JG 3 had scrambled from Schafstädt. The Fw 190 pilots first rendezvoused with their escort (provided by the Bf 109s of JG 4's other three *Gruppen*) before being vectored westwards towards Magdeburg. They encountered the enemy some 20 miles (32 km) to the southeast of the town, and were immediately pounced upon by hordes of vigilant Mustangs.

Once again it was the covering Bf 109s that bore the brunt of the enemy's fury. This allowed several of IV. *Gruppe's Sturmböcke* to get through to the Fortresses and claim at least four of their number. In return, IV.(*Sturm*)/JG 4 sustained eight combat casualties – five pilots killed or missing and three wounded. This represented over half of the unit's attacking force.

The heavy *Sturm* losses of 2 November – which included two *Staffelkapitäne* – resulted in another relatively quiet three weeks as yet more replacement men and machines arrived to fill the gaps. Two new *Staffelkapitäne* were appointed, neither of whom would last long. Towards the end of this period a seventh serving member of the *Sturm* force was awarded the Knight's Cross. This was the *Kapitän* of 5.(*Sturm*)/JG 300, Leutnant Klaus Bretschneider, who received the decoration on 18 November for an overall total of 31 victories (14 of them by night during JG 300's earlier employment as a *'Wilde Sau'* unit) culminating in his recent remarkable treble.

ANTI-*JABO* OPERATIONS

On 19 November IV.(*Sturm*)/JG 3 and II.(*Sturm*)/JG 4 were ordered to vacate their bases in central Germany and transfer westwards, the former to Störmede, southeast of Osnabrück, and the latter to Babenhausen, down near Frankfurt. While II.(*Sturm*)/JG 300 remained at Löbnitz, deep within the Reich, the other two *Sturmgruppens'* move had inevitably taken them much closer to the ground fighting on the western front. The reason for their transfer was soon made clear. Not only were they to continue their long-running campaign against the Eighth Air Force's high-altitude bombers, they would also be expected to fly low-level missions in pursuit of the Allied fighter-bombers now marauding almost at will over much of western Germany.

Things did not get off to a good start. On 26 November, after days of heavy rain, IV.(*Sturm*)/JG 3 was instructed to scramble, no matter what, to attack enemy fighter-bombers reported over the Ruhr area. Despite the appalling conditions – visibility less than a kilometre (1750 yards) and the cloud base down to 75 metres (250 ft) – Major Moritz attempted to comply. But several of the heavy *Sturmböcke*, including the *Kommandeur's* own, became firmly stuck in the boggy surface of the field while taxiing out. Take-off was clearly impossible.

At nearby Lippstadt the Bf 109s of I./JG 3 *had* managed to get off the ground, only to lose their recently appointed *Gruppenkommandeur*, Hauptmann Horst Haase, in a mid-air collision. The lead was taken over by Leutnant Walter Brandt, the highly experienced *Staffelkapitän* of 2./JG 3, but after finding no trace of the enemy, he broke off the mission and ordered a return to base. The foray had cost the *Gruppe* three pilots killed and five Messerschmitts lost – proof, if any were needed, of the atrocious weather in the region at the time.

Further members of 5.(*Sturm*)/JG 300 are seen in November 1944. They are, from left to right, Unteroffizier Schröder, Oberfeldwebel Winter, Oberfähnrich Piel, Oberleutnant Maier (a gunnery instructor), Leutnant Graziadei, Oberfähnrich Schneider and Fahnenjunker-Oberfeldwebel Löfgen. Of these seven pilots, only two (Schröder and Graziadei) would survive the last six months of the war

Veteran *Sturm* pilot Leutnant Siegfried Müller saw considerable action from mid-1943 until war's end. Having initially been sent to II./JG 51 in Sardinia in mid 1943, he volunteered for service with *Sturmstaffel* 1 in March 1944. Subsequently flying with 16. and 13.(*Sturm*)/JG 3, Müller was posted to Me 262-equipped JG 7 in April 1945. A rare *Sturm* survivor, he had claimed 17 kills by war's end.

There are many photos of Unteroffizier Schröder's *Kölle alaaf!*, but few show 'Red 19's' starboard side, which bore the name of his girlfriend Edelgard. This picture was taken on 25 November, just 48 hours before 'Red 19' was written-off . . .

Nevertheless, after landing back at Lippstadt, Leutnant Brandt found himself facing a court martial for failing to carry out orders. Major Moritz was threatened with the same, but saner minds then prevailed. He was, however, warned to expect a posting to a training unit in the very near future.

The next day (27 November) IV.(*Sturm*)/JG 3 went up against its old adversaries of the Eighth Air Force, which was out in significant numbers attacking transportation targets. Led on this occasion by Leutnant Siegfried Müller, the *Gruppe* was unable to break through the strong screen of escorting fighters. The Fw 190 pilots were fortunate to get back to Störmede without serious loss.

Further to the east, II.(*Sturm*)/JG 300 was not so fortunate. Its pilots, who were also part of a large *Gefechtsverband* led by Oberstleutnant Walther Dahl, were set upon by the now seemingly ever-present Mustangs. In a series of wide-ranging dogfights over the Halberstadt-Quedlinburg area – the scene of so many *Sturm* assaults in the past – the *Gruppe* lost seven pilots killed and four wounded. 5. *Staffel's* Unteroffizier Ernst Schröder was very nearly one of them. With a damaged rudder, and unable to turn, he was attempting to escape at low level when;

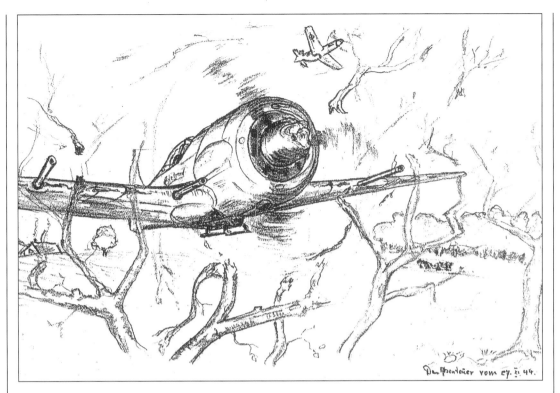

Der Abenteuer vom 27. XI. 44.

... and this is Ernst Schröder's own sketch of the incident which hastened its demise as, harried by a Mustang, he unintentionally ploughs through the top of a large tree!

'Suddenly a bare metal P-51, looking brand new, appeared just above to my left. I could clearly see the pilot peering down at me from his large glass canopy. He obviously didn't want to overshoot and get ahead of me, so using his excess of speed he pulled up and away to port.

'I could no longer see him but, expecting him to attack at any second, I nearly dislocated my neck trying to look behind me. When I glanced forward again, the edge of a forest of large trees was filling my windscreen. I heaved back on the stick, but there was an almighty crash as my *"Bock"* tore through the top branches of a huge tree at something over 500 km/h (310 mph). My cockpit immediately filled with blue smoke as I carefully tried to gain enough height to bale out.'

In fact, Unteroffizier Schröder managed to belly-land his machine on a nearby airfield. It was a sorry sight. The spinner and wing leading-edges looked as if they had been 'attacked with an axe', there were at least 25 bullet holes in the wings and fuselage, and lumps of tree were found embedded in the radiator. It was the end of the road for Schröder's well-known 'Red 19' *Kölle alaaf!*.

The Luftwaffe lost over 50 fighters that day. They had not brought down a single heavy bomber!

The following day (28 November), IV.(*Sturm*)/JG 3, back hunting fighter-bombers at low level, managed to claim a brace of Mustangs near Aachen. And 72 hours after that a single P-51 provided the first victory for Hauptmann Hubert-York Weydenhammer, the *Staffelkapitän* of 15.(*Sturm*)/JG 3.

Then came 2 December.

That day's targets for the Eighth's 'heavies' were marshalling yards along a 37-mile (60 km) stretch of the Rhine between Koblenz and Bingen.

Scrambled from Störmede shortly before midday, IV.(*Sturm*)/JG 3 was vectored almost due south towards the B-24s of the 2nd Bomb Division, heading for Bingen. The Fw 190 pilots intercepted the formation of 130+ Liberators, escorted by an even larger number of P-51s, while it was still on its approach west of the Rhine.

IV.(*Sturm*)/JG 3's own fighter cover (the Bf 109s of I. and III./JG 3) suffered a severe mauling in opening up a path through to the bombers, but their sacrifice (over a dozen pilots killed, others wounded, and 16 machines lost) paved the way for the last major *Sturm* assault of the war.

The *Sturmböcke* hit the B-24s over the rolling countryside between the Moselle and Rhine rivers to the southwest of Koblenz. In less than ten minutes they claimed 22 Liberators. This was exactly double the Eighth Air Force's admitted losses but, again, the inexperience of many of the *Gruppe's* young replacements pilots may partly explain this over-claiming in the heat of battle – no fewer than 13 of the credited kills were firsts.

For two of the claimants, their first victories were also to be their last. After attacking the bombers, it was the Focke-Wulfs' turn to run the gauntlet of US fighters – and not just those of the B-24s' immediate escort, but also the many others flying general sweeps of the Rhineland area now hastening to the scene of the action. Ten Fw 190s were shot down or written-off in crash landings, and at least four more were damaged. Five pilots were killed and two wounded.

This engagement effectively marked the demise of Major Hans-Günter von Kornatzki's *Sturm* idea. Three days later, as if to underline the fact, Major Wilhelm Moritz relinquished command of the Luftwaffe's original *Sturmgruppe*. He would see out most of the remainder of the war at the

Some of IV.(*Sturm*)/JG 3's machines retained their 'blinkers' right up until the end of the *Gruppe's Sturm* career, as evidenced by Unteroffizier Oskar Bösch's 'Black 14', pictured at Schafstädt in the late autumn of 1944

head of a training unit. The official reason for his departure was given as 'combat exhaustion', and this may not have been far off the mark.

IV.(*Sturm*)/JG 3 was not only the Luftwaffe's *first Sturmgruppe*, it was also by far the most successful, and Wilhelm Moritz had been at its head throughout. Many of the surviving pilots who served under him still remember the quiet but authoritative *'Pauke, Pauke!'* ('Attack, Attack!') call in their headphones as he led them into yet another assault on the seemingly endless streams of US heavy bombers.

Since its return from the misguided venture into France at the time of the Normandy invasion, IV.(*Sturm*)/JG 3 had been credited with the destruction of some 270 of those four-engined enemy bombers. But its successes had cost the unit well over half that number of Fw 190s, together with 76 pilots killed or missing and a further 44 wounded or injured.

The beginning of December also spelled the end of the road for II.(*Sturm*)/JG 4 as a dedicated bomber-killer *Gruppe*. According to one pilot, as soon as the unit received the order to transfer to Babenhausen for western front operations, the mechanics immediately started to remove the *Sturmböckes'* heavy armour-plating and outboard 30 mm wing cannon to convert them into 'light' fighters.

Although, according to pilots' log-books, the appellation *'Sturm'* would remain in use right up until the final surrender, it was only II.(*Sturm*)/JG 300 – from its base at Löbnitz, in central Germany, about 75 miles (120 km) to the south-southwest of Berlin – which would continue to operate primarily in the anti-bomber role. And even it rarely, if ever, flew the true, massed *Sturm*-type assaults to which the Eighth and Fifteenth Air Forces had been subjected during the five months from July to December 1944. The opposition was simply too overwhelming.

Here is 'Black 14' again – note the broad wooden propeller blades – shortly before the *Gruppe's* move to Störmede on 19 November. This photograph reflects even more starkly the almost unimaginable odds facing the Luftwaffe's young fighter pilots during the final six months of the war. Of the 13 pictured here, ten would be reported killed or missing, one would be wounded, and just two – including Oskar Bösch (second right) – would come through unscathed

THE BULGE, *BODENPLATTE* AND THE END IN THE EAST

The *Sturm* experiment was over. After November 1944 II.(*Sturm*)/JG 4, operating almost exclusively in the tactical role, would not claim another four-engined heavy bomber. For IV.(*Sturm*)/JG 3, there was one last major confrontation with the Eighth Air Force yet to come. Only the Fw 190s of II.(*Sturm*)/JG 300, together with the other *Gruppen* of its parent *Geschwader* and those of JG 301, remained as the sole daylight defenders of the Reich until they too were drawn into supporting the ground forces at war's end.

Although that war still had six months to run, the outcome was no longer in any doubt. The Allied armies that had landed in Normandy were now closing in on the Reich's western borders – Aachen, the first major German city to be captured, had fallen to the Americans on 21 October. In the east the Red Army was preparing for the offensive that would take it to the gates of Berlin.

But the Führer had one last ploy up his sleeve – a bold, many said foolhardy, but inevitably disastrous counter-offensive through the Ardennes. The roles played by the two western-based *Sturmgruppen* in the 'Battle of the Bulge' and its aftermath are not really part of the story of Major von Kornatzki's original *Sturm* concept, but they warrant a brief description here if only because they resulted in the loss of several familiar names.

On 16 December 1944 – the day the surprise Ardennes counter-attack was launched – IV.(*Sturm*)/JG 3 made the short 17-mile (27 km) hop northwards from Störmede to Gütersloh, which was to be its base for the next six weeks. Twenty-four hours later both IV.(*Sturm*)/JG 3 and II.(*Sturm*)/JG 4 found themselves in action against US fighters over the battle area. One of the former's six claims – a P-47 brought down west of Bonn – was credited to Wolfgang Kosse. It was kill number 25 for Kosse, the ex-*Sturmstaffel* 1 pilot, now fully rehabilitated, restored to the rank of hauptmann and serving as *Kapitän* of 13.(*Sturm*)/JG 3.

Closer to the Belgian border, II.(*Sturm*)/JG 4 lost five of its 'lightened' *Sturmböcke* and had three pilots killed without itself gaining a single victory.

Meanwhile, far to the east over Olmütz (Olomouc), in Czechoslovakia, on this same 17 December, Major Alfred Lindenberger was leading II.(*Sturm*)/JG 300 into an attack on a force of Fifteenth Air Force B-24s reportedly heading for a synthetic-oil plant in Poland. The *Gruppe* claimed 22 Liberators and a single P-38 escort in little more than ten minutes (shades of times past!), but only at the cost of seven of its own pilots killed and three wounded.

Bad weather over the western front during the next 48 hours severely restricted operations, but failed to prevent the loss of three more II.(*Sturm*)/JG 4 pilots in action over the Rhine region. Then, on 23 December, the fog and low cloud that Hitler had gambled upon to protect his ground forces from air attack as they advanced through the Ardennes finally lifted. Under an almost cloudless pale blue winter sky, the Eighth and Ninth Air Forces turned out in strength to support the hard-pressed US troops below.

Shortly after 1100 hrs, II.(*Sturm*)/JG 4 was scrambled from Babenhausen to intercept a formation of high-flying B-17s heading for railway supply lines behind the German front. Setting course towards Trier, the Fw 190 pilots were still climbing when they were jumped by Mustangs. Without even getting through to the bombers, a dozen *Sturmböcke* were shot down or forced to break away damaged. Six pilots, all of 8. *Staffel*, were reported killed or missing. A seventh was wounded.

IV.(*Sturm*)/JG 3 had lifted off from Gütersloh at almost the same time. It too was directed towards a force of Eighth Air Force 'heavies' apparently making for rail targets to the rear of the battle area. Before gaining contact with the bombers, however, the *Gruppe* came across a roving band of P-47s west of Bonn, three of which were shot down in a brief but vicious dogfight.

Only a minute or so later a large formation of twin-engined Marauders was sighted. These are believed to have been machines of the 386th and 391st BGs (see *Osprey Combat Aircraft 2 – B-26 Marauder Units of the Eighth and Ninth Air Forces* for further details), aiming for the Ahrweiler railway viaduct just west of the Rhine. Having failed to meet up with its fighter escort, the lead group of B-26s was completely unprotected as it commenced its bomb run. It was at this moment that the Fw 190s struck.

A mechanic runs up the engine of Leutnant Klaus Bretschneider's 'Red 1' under the cover of trees at Löbnitz in early December 1944

While II.(*Sturm*)/JG 300 remained on Defence of the Reich duties throughout the closing weeks of 1944, the other two *Sturmgruppen* had transferred closer to the western front. Here they faced new opposition – the machines of the tactical Ninth Air Force, including P-47Ds such as those of the 362nd FG seen taking off here . . .

Marauder crewmen later described coming under attack from some 60 Luftwaffe fighters, which hurled themselves at the B-26s in four separate waves 15 abreast. Sixteen of the leading 391st BG's aircraft alone went down over the target area. In just eight minutes IV.(*Sturm*)/JG 3 was credited with the destruction of no fewer than 30 of the twin-engined bombers! The day's cost to the *Gruppe* was six fighters shot down, with two pilots killed and one wounded.

The following day, Christmas Eve 1944, the *Gruppe* was again sent up to intercept a force of approaching Eighth Air Force 'heavies'. This time, after a good hour in the air, they found them – nearing Liège, in Belgium.

. . . and B-26 Marauders. IV.(*Sturm*)/ JG 3 was credited with destroying no fewer than 30 of these twin-engined bombers close to the Rhine on 23 December

IV.(*Sturm*)/JG 3 had rarely, if ever, engaged the enemy outside the borders of the Reich, but Hauptmann Hubert-York Weydenhammer, who had assumed command of the *Gruppe* after Major Moritz's departure, immediately gave the order to attack.

From a position behind and slightly below their opponents IV.(*Sturm*)/JG 3 – for the last time in its history – bored in towards a box of Eighth Air Force Fortresses. The Fw 190 pilots claimed eight of the B-17s, plus two *Herausschüsse*, which tallies neatly with the ten aircraft of the 487th BG that failed to return from Mission No 760. Six Focke-Wulfs were shot down in the Liège area, with one pilot being killed and the remaining five baling out into Allied captivity.

But the day's successes, and losses, did not end there. Having re-formed, the *Gruppe* had just set out back to base when it chanced upon a gaggle of Typhoons and shot four of them down. The Hawker fighters were the *Gruppe's* first kills over the RAF (although two of the victims may actually have been the machines of No 440 Sqn RCAF reportedly lost to Fw 190s southeast of Eindhoven) since its days in Italy. Three Fw 190s had also gone down in the melée, and two of the pilots later returned to Gütersloh unharmed. Hauptmann Wolfgang Kosse, who had just been credited with two of the Typhoons to bring his final total to 28, remained missing.

II.(*Sturm*)/JG 4 had an even more eventful, and far less successful, Christmas Eve. Not only was the *Gruppe* bounced by enemy fighters over the Rhine Valley while en route to the Ardennes battle front, costing it four *Sturmböcke* shot down and two pilots killed, the unit's own Babenhausen base was the day's target for a force of almost 100 B-17s of the Eighth Air Force's 3rd Bomb Division. Although the runway was 'literally ploughed up', damage to machines and casualties among personnel was fortunately limited.

On Christmas Eve 1944, IV.(*Sturm*)/JG 3 achieved its last major success against the Eighth Air Force's heavy bombers, claiming ten Fortresses of the 487th BG over Belgium. One of the group's B-17Gs aloft that day was the 838th BS's *High Tailed Lady*, which made it safely back to Lavenham

The *Kapitän* of 5.(*Sturm*)/JG 300, Leutnant Klaus Bretschneider, was killed in a dogfight with P-51s on 24 December. He went down in *Rauhbautz VII* somewhere near Kassel

Other Fortresses of the 1st Bomb Division had, meanwhile, been hitting airfields in the Giessen area, only to be threatened themselves on their return flight by the Focke-Wulfs of II.(*Sturm*)/JG 300. With Major Peters incapacitated by a leg wound, the *Gruppe* was being led on this occasion by the experienced Leutnant Klaus Bretschneider, Kapitän of 5. *Staffel*. But the departing B-17s were well served by their escorting Mustangs, who took a heavy toll of the would-be attackers. In a series of separate dogfights stretching from Kassel to Göttingen, II.(*Sturm*)/JG 300 lost six pilots killed and seven wounded. Among the former was Knight's Cross holder Klaus Bretschneider.

Exactly one week later, on New Year's Eve, II.(*Sturm*)/JG 300 again suffered considerable casualties – another six pilots killed, plus three wounded – when the Eighth Air Force returned to its strategic bombing campaign by striking at oil and industrial targets in the far north of Germany. Despite, or perhaps because of, these losses, the New Year's party back at Löbnitz, attended by wives, girlfriends and other guests,

Two of Klaus Bretschneider's pilots who were both wounded shortly after the loss of their *Staffelkapitän* – Leutnant Norbert Graziadei who, as *Staffelführer* (formation leader in the air) was at the head of 5.(*Sturm*)/JG 300 when he was brought down east of Bremen on New Year's Eve 1944 . . .

went on well into the early hours. There would, however, be no such festivities for the two western-bound *Sturmgruppen*.

After the bombing of 24 December, things had remained fairly quiet for II.(*Sturm*)/JG 4 at Babenhausen while the field was being restored to operational use. But for IV.(*Sturm*)/JG 3, it had been business as usual. On Christmas Day, 20 of the *Gruppe's Sturmböcke* were sent up against a force of Eighth Air Force Liberators approaching the Ardennes battleground. Interception again took place over Belgium, but only a single B-24 was brought down.

In return, IV.(*Sturm*)/JG 3 lost nine machines to the bombers' strong escort of P-51s. Five pilots were killed or missing and another two ended up in PoW camps. One of the two known fatalities was Hauptmann Hubert-York Weydenhammer – the unit's *Gruppenkommandeur* for all of 20 days – whose 'Black Chevron 5' went down somewhere between Liège and St Vith.

The four Ninth Air Force P-47 Thunderbolts also claimed on this date were scant recompense for the *Gruppe's* own losses. Nor were the

. . . and Unteroffizier Matthäus Erhardt, who baled out of his stricken machine on 14 January 1945 during the last great aerial battle of the Defence of the Reich campaign

two victories of 27 December, one of them a four-engined bomber (believed to have been a B-17) destroyed either by deliberate ramming or in a mid-air collision, for by this time another seven pilots killed or missing had been added to IV.(*Sturm*)/JG 3's ever-lengthening list of casualties. Fortunately, perhaps, the weather then closed in again and the last four days of 1944 saw little further activity for the *Gruppe*.

All the more surprising, therefore, that New Year's Eve celebrations were banned and the pilots of IV.(*Sturm*)/JG 3 and II.(*Sturm*)/JG 4 ordered to turn in early. The reason for these seemingly killjoy measures was revealed during the next morning's briefings at Luftwaffe fighter fields throughout western Germany.

The 'Big Blow' was finally on, but not as the *General der Jagdflieger* had envisaged it. Despite the inroads made into his carefully hoarded fighter strength by the past weeks' operations over the Ardennes, more than 900 machines were being readied for a massed assault on the enemy. Much to Galland's disgust, however, the target was not to be one of the Eighth Air Force's mighty bomber streams. His plans had been overridden by higher authority and his pilots were being sent instead to carry out low-level attacks on bases of the Allied tactical air forces in the Low Countries and France.

The story of the New Year's Day operation, code-named *Bodenplatte* ('Base plate'), has been told in great detail elsewhere. Suffice it here to say that, of the two *Sturmgruppen* involved, IV.(*Sturm*)/JG 3 was by far the more successful.

The *Gruppe's* target was Eindhoven, an airfield in Holland that was currently housing eight squadrons of Typhoons, three of Spitfires and sundry other units. After scrambling from Gütersloh shortly before 0830

Sturmstaffel 1 veteran Leutnant Siegfried Müller led IV.(*Sturm*)/JG 3 during *Bodenplatte*. This photograph of the fighter ace was taken in March 1945, his flying jacket adorned with a 'Whites-of-the-Eyes' emblem

hrs, the Focke-Wulfs of IV.(*Sturm*)/JG 3 first rendezvoused with the Bf 109s of I. and III./JG 3 over Lippstadt, before setting course almost due east for Eindhoven. The *Gruppe* was led by Leutnant Siegfried Müller, another ex-*Sturmstaffel* 1 veteran and now, as *Staffelführer* of 16.(*Sturm*)/JG 3, one of the unit's most experienced pilots.

Going about its normal morning duties, Eindhoven was taken almost completely by surprise. It is, of course, impossible to be certain how many of the 100 or so Allied machines destroyed or damaged on the ground were accounted for by the *Gruppe's* Fw 190s. What *is* known is that they claimed a brace each of Typhoons and Spitfires in the air. Their own casualties, suffered mainly over the target area and on the return flight, were seven machines lost, four pilots killed or missing and one PoW.

JG 4's FAILURE

If JG 3's strike against Eindhoven was the success story of the day, JG 4's attempt to emulate their performance at Le Culot, in Belgium, was a total and costly failure. For II.(*Sturm*)/JG 4 things got off to a bad start when one of its *Sturmböcke* crashed on take-off from Babenhausen. The others met up with I. and IV./JG 4s Bf 109s over the Rhine and then headed northwest across the Eifel hills towards the Belgian border.

They were greeted over enemy territory by heavy and accurate anti-aircraft fire, and more aircraft were lost. The formation became scattered, and it appears that not a single pilot managed to even locate, let alone attack, Le Culot. Several tacked themselves onto other units as JG 4's mission unravelled into chaos. With nearly half its aircraft failing to return, JG 4's was the highest casualty rate of all the 11 *Jagdgeschwader* participating in *Bodenplatte*.

US Army GIs look over the remains of one of the twelve II.(*Sturm***)/JG 4 machines that failed to return from Operation** ***Bodenplatte*** . . .

. . . while another of the 12 Fw 190s lost would gain considerable notoriety by belly-landing in the middle of a USAAF fighter airfield! The resident 404th FG quickly got Gefreiter Walter Wagner's 'White 11' back on its feet . . .

. . . and then proceeded to give it a whole new paint job – red overall, with prominent USAAF stars and bars!

II.(*Sturm*)/JG 4 alone lost 11 aircraft, with five pilots killed or missing, two wounded and three in captivity. All the unit had to show for it was a single Auster shot down.

Bodenplatte proved to be the aerial equivalent of the Führer's ill-judged ground counter-offensive in the Ardennes – a last-throw gamble that failed to come off. Worse, it dealt a mortal blow to the *Jagdwaffe*. The operation's total cost of over 200 pilots, many of them experienced formation leaders, could no longer be made good.

Some measures were taken to restore a semblance of order. On 5 January, for example, IV.(*Sturm*)/JG 3 received a new *Kommandeur* to

replace the fallen Hauptmann Weydenhammer. It was none other than Major Erwin Bacsila, but he would remain in office little more than a month. The *Gruppe* would see three more changes of command before the war's end.

For the first two weeks of the new year there had been little activity. Then came the last major confrontation between the Eighth Air Force and the Luftwaffe fighters defending the Reich. Mission No 792 of 14 January was directed once again at Germany's by now almost non-existent oil producing industry. Once again the *Jagdgruppen* rose to the challenge, but by now most were just shadows of their former selves, particularly the one-time *Sturm* units.

At Babenhausen, the inexperience of II.(*Sturm*)/JG 4's replacement pilots had led the *Geschwaderkommodore* of JG 4 to restrict them to local operations only. Gütersloh saw IV.(*Sturm*)/JG 3 put just 12 machines into the air under the leadership of Feldwebel Oskar Bösch. Trying to get through to the bombers, the Focke-Wulfs were jumped over the German-Dutch border and all 12 were shot down. Four pilots were killed and an equal number wounded.

Closer to the bombers' objectives in central Germany, it then became the turn of JGs 300 and 301 to challenge the near total domination of the escorting P-51s. The attempt cost them 54 pilots killed and 15 wounded! Up from Löbnitz, II.(*Sturm*)/JG 300 counted itself one of the luckier *Gruppen* with just seven casualties.

Altogether, 14 January 1945 ended with the loss of 107 pilots killed or missing, plus another 32 wounded. It was the final nail in the coffin of the Defence of the Reich campaign. Putting all thoughts of the Ardennes behind him, the Führer now ordered the bulk of the daylight fighter force to be transferred to the eastern front, where the Soviets were already closing up on the River Oder – the last great natural barrier before Berlin.

It was in the east that the former *Sturmgruppen* would continue the fight until the very end, still trying to stop an unstoppable foe – no longer the endless streams of heavy bombers parading high across Germany's skies,

Feldwebel Oskar Bösch led 12 Fw 190s of IV.(*Sturm*)/JG 3 into the air on 14 January 1945 and *all* were shot down by P-51s. Only Feldwebel Bösch and three others escaped unhurt

Machines of II.(*Sturm*)/JG 300 display their new blue-white-blue Defence of the Reich bands at Löbnitz in early 1945

On 17 February 1945 Oberleutnant Oskar Romm was appointed *Gruppenkommandeur* of IV.(*Sturm*)/JG 3. He is pictured here (centre) in early April with his three *Staffelkapitäne* – from left to right, Leutnant Siegfried Müller (13.), an admin officer, 'Ossi' Romm, Leutnant Karl-Dieter Hecker (15.) and Leutnant Willi Unger (14.). 16. *Staffel* had been disbanded in mid-March

Although employed exclusively at low level against the Red Air Force in the east for the final three months of the war, IV./JG 3 was still being referred to as a *Sturm* unit, as is confirmed by the last of the postings listed in this pilot's *Wehrpass*. The bottom line reads, '26.4.45 – 2.5.45, IV *Sturm*/J.G. Udet, 13. *Staffel*'. On the latter date the *Gruppe* was to fly to Westerland, on the island of Sylt, to surrender to the RAF

II.(*Sturm*)/JG 300 ended its days in the southern half of the by now divided Germany, but the exact location of the last resting place of 8. *Staffel's* 'Black 12' is not known

but the flood-tide of Red Army tank and infantry units bearing down on the nation's capital.

Those closing weeks of the war on the Oder front, with the *Gruppen* able to send only a handful of aircraft out at a time to carry out low-level attacks on concentrations of enemy troops and armour, were just about as far removed from Major von Kornatzki's original high-altitude, massed *Sturm* assault concept as it was possible to get. Yet, even now, there were still some familiar names harking back to the early days of the great experiment.

On 14 April 1945 – with surrender now just over three weeks away – Major Wilhelm Moritz, released from his training duties by the disbandment of IV./EJG 1, took over from Major Gerhard Schroeder as the last *Gruppenkommandeur* of II.(*Sturm*)/JG 4. The following day 14.(*Sturm*)/JG 3's Feldwebel Willi Maximowitz claimed his final two victories (a pair of Soviet Yak-3s) to the east of Berlin. Forty-eight hours after that, Feldwebel Maximowitz and his *Schwarm* were last seen in a furious dogfight with Red Air Force fighters in the same area. Not one of the four Focke-Wulfs returned.

II.(*Sturm*)/JG 4 flew its final ops against the Russians on the Oder front. To escape possible Soviet captivity, two of the *Gruppe's* pilots – both Estonian volunteers – flew to neutral Sweden. 'Black 10' (still bearing the unit badge) was landed by Oberfähnrich Axel Kessler at Bulltofta on 19 April

POSTSCRIPT – FROM *STURM* TO *RAMM*

There have been many misconceptions about the true nature of the Luftwaffe's *Sturmgruppen*. Some sources have referred to them as punishment units, akin to the German army's penal battalions. Others maintained that they were straightforward 'kamikaze'-style suicide units. Both descriptions are demonstrably false.

Towards the later stages of the war, and particularly during its closing chaotic days, there actually *were* a number of small SO units (SO standing for *Selbstopfer*, literally self-sacrifice, or suicide), among them the earlier *Sonderstaffeln* (Special squadrons) 'Einhorn' and 'Leonidas', and the SO-*Gruppen* A and B. Fighter cover for the latter pair, whose pilots dived their bomb-carrying single-seaters into the Oder bridges in an effort to halt the Red Army's advance on Berlin, was often provided by the Bf 109s of JG 4.

Most of these SO units were the brainchild of ideologists within the Nazi Party, and most of their volunteer members either fanatics or true idealists. But perhaps the most famous 'suicide' unit of all, which, in the strictest terms, it was not, was a product of calculated military expediency. The man behind it was the same Hajo Herrmann, now promoted to Oberst, who had proposed the original *'Wilde Sau'* nightfighter scheme.

Having risen in the meantime to the position of Inspectorate of Aerial Defence, Herrmann was just as aware as *General der Jagdflieger* Adolf Galland that the *Sturmgruppen* had been unable to produce their intended result. With Galland's own 'Big Blow' having come to nought, Oberst Herrmann's plan was to take the *Sturm* concept one logical step further still. He wanted to form an all-volunteer fighter unit that would undertake to carry out a massed attack on a USAAF heavy bomber formation not using cannon, with ramming as a last resort, but with the intention from the outset deliberately to ram.

As a sop to the sensibilities of the more conservatively minded in the OKL, it was pointed out that this would *not* be a suicide mission. Great stress was laid upon the fact that the pilot had every chance of surviving a mid-air collision, as witness the many previous instances of *Sturm* pilots having done just that. But as the volunteers would be flying standard Bf 109 fighters rather than heavily armoured *Sturmböcke*, the odds on survival would not be high!

Despite more than a little opposition, the plan was finally approved. A top-secret teletext, drafted by Oberst Herrmann and signed by *Reichsmarschall* Göring, went out on 8 March 1945. It did not go via the usual channels, but was addressed directly to the Kommodores of all fighter, nightfighter and fighter training *Geschwader* within the *Luftflotte Reich*.

Under conditions of the strictest secrecy, the recipients were ordered to read the contents to all operational pilots and those nearing completion of their training. The first part was a stirring call to arms;

If Major von Kornatzki had been the 'Father of the *Sturm* Idea', Oberst Hajo Herrmann (pictured here as a Major) was very much the driving force behind the ramming tactics to be employed by *Kommando* Elbe

'The final battle to decide the fate of the Reich, our *Volk* and our Homeland has reached its climax. Almost the entire world is ranged in battle against us and is determined to destroy us. With every last ounce of strength we are standing up to this threatening tide. As never before in the history of our German Fatherland, we are being threatened with a final destruction from which there can be no resurrection. This danger can only be averted by the utmost use of the highest ideals of the German warrior. I therefore turn to you at this decisive moment. Risk your lives to rescue the nation from defeat! I am calling upon you to undertake a mission from which there is only a limited chance of your returning. Those of you who volunteer will be sent for further training.

'Comrades, yours will be the place of honour alongside the most famous heroes of the Luftwaffe. You will give the entire German *Volk* hope in its hour of greatest danger, and be an example for all time.'

There followed instructions that the numbers of those volunteering should be submitted itemised by individual unit, but that names should

119

Major Otto Köhnke had flown as a bomber pilot with KG 54 'Totenkopf' before being severely wounded and losing a leg. A succession of staff appointments ultimately led to his taking command of *Kommando* Elbe

also be appended so that these latter 'can be held up as shining examples of heroic action'.

Some 2,000 pilots answered the appeal. The great majority came direct from training schools, although at least one operational *Jagdgruppe* reportedly volunteered *en bloc*. Significantly, perhaps, there were very few takers from the ranks of the ex-*Sturmgruppen*.

Their numbers, however, were greatly reduced when Oberst Herrmann learned that the 1,000 Bf 109s he had requested for the mission would not be forthcoming. He was at first promised 350, but finally had to settle for something just over half that total. Most of the machines made available would be new-build late model Bf 109Gs and Ks straight from the production lines.

On 24 March 184 pilots arrived at Stendal, an airfield about 55 miles (88 km) to the west of Berlin. Here, they officially became known as the *Schulungslehrgang* (Training course) Elbe, although this was later shortened simply to *Kommando* Elbe.

The only Knight's Cross holder to volunteer for the *Kommando* was Hauptmann Ernst Sorge, who had won the award as a reconnaissance pilot on the Arctic front (he is shown here after completing 200 operational flights). *Reichsmarschall* Göring, however, had expressly ordered that no highly experienced, highly decorated pilots be accepted. But when requested to step down, Sorge asked how it would look if the unit's sole Knight's Cross wearer decided to 'pack up and go home'. He was allowed to fly, and survived a crash-landing

Under the leadership of Major Otto Köhnke, a Knight's Cross-wearing ex-bomber pilot and now head of the Inspectorate of A/B Training Schools, the ten-day course of instruction at Stendal was purely theoretical. Among the experts brought in to explain the mechanics of a successful ramming attack – strike at the bomber's aft fuselage immediately ahead of the tail – was one Willi Maximowitz!

A similar course was being held outside Prague, where further volunteers had been gathered on three fields near the Czech capital. These were mainly pilots from bomber units awaiting conversion to Me 262

jets, and were apparently intended primarily as back-up on the day of the action should the Eighth Air Force bomber streams, currently targeting northern Germany on an almost daily basis, make an unexpected change of course to the southeast.

Tuition at Stendal came to an end on 4 April. About a dozen volunteers remained on the base, together with some 50 Fw 190 pilots who were scheduled to fly cover for the mission (in the event, not a single Focke-Wulf was delivered and the attack would be carried out unescorted).

The main body of volunteers, divided into four groups of 30-40 each, were ferried by road to the bases from which they would be taking off – Gardelegen and Sachau, both fairly close to Stendal, and Delitzsch and Mörtitz, some distance further away to the northeast of Leipzig. Here, the four groups, further sub-divided into *Schwärme* and *Rotten* (operational formations of four and two aircraft respectively), were introduced to the machines they were going to fly.

The mission was to be flown at very high altitude. In order to save weight, most of the Messerschmitts had their heavy engine-mounted cannon removed. Many had at least one of their fuselage machine guns taken out as well, leaving just a single weapon and 60 rounds in the magazine – the pilot of one such machine subsequently claimed to have shot down a heavy bomber! Some reports suggest that the Prague units flew aircraft that were completely unarmed.

Having drawn heated flying suits and other high altitude gear, a number of pilots requested permission to make at least one test flight to get the feel of their brand new and untried mounts. But this was refused due to the shortage of fuel (some of the available machines even had to be drained to provide sufficient fuel for the others).

The date selected for the operation was 7 April 1945. It was a day of maximum effort by the Eighth Air Force, which despatched all three divisions – more than 1300 bombers in total, plus a fighter escort of some 850 aircraft – against a whole range of marshalling yards, airfields and other targets in northern Germany.

The *Kommando* Elbe units received orders to take off shortly after 1100 hrs. The Stendal and Gardelegen groups, together numbering about 60 fighters, were instructed to meet up over Dömitz, on the River Elbe to the east of Lüneburg, and there gain height while awaiting confirmation of the bombers' exact heading. Meanwhile, the Sachau group flew southeast to the Magdeburg area, where it was to rendezvous with the force flying up from Leipzig.

After nearly an hour in the air, their headphones filled with martial music interspersed with exhortations from a female controller, it was – appropriately enough – the formation which had climbed to some 36,000 ft (11,000 m) above the Elbe which first made contact with the enemy. Unfortunately, that contact was with the bombers' strong escorting force of P-51 and P-47 fighters.

For many of the inexperienced young Luftwaffe pilots, flying together in small groups, the mission ended right there. Large numbers were shot down. Others, their machines damaged, sought to escape by diving away. But a determined few managed to get through to the B-24s. High above Lüneburg Heath they hurled themselves at the Liberators. There have been several attempts to separate and describe the individual actions that occurred during the next chaotic 45 minutes or more.

Training machines found abandoned in Czechoslovakia after the end of the war. Bf 109s such as these would have provided the back-up force for *Kommando* Elbe

One source speaks of the lead Liberator being rammed and going down, taking a wingman with it. Another pilot recounts how his Bf 109 chopped the tail off one B-24 and was catapulted into the wing of a second, which then collided with a third. But, although many bombers staggered back to bases in France and the UK with large parts of their tails and sections of wings missing, records indicate that only three were actually brought down.

Meanwhile, the formations that had rendezvoused over Magdeburg were climbing steadily north-westwards (with two-dozen Bf 109G-14s up from Prague paralleling their course some miles to the south) towards a 500-strong force of B-17s. Battle was joined shortly after midday to the north of Hannover. In a repetition of events just played out above Lüneburg, the single-gunned (or completely unarmed) Messerschmitts had to run the gauntlet of the Fortresses' strong fighter escort. Those that succeeded in doing so then dived unhesitatingly on the B-17s.

Again, there are accounts of stricken bombers going down and taking others with them. This force certainly suffered more than the B-24s, losing 14 Fortresses, with many times that number damaged. But this did not prevent the Eighth Air Force from bombing its assigned targets. Like the *Sturmgruppen* before it, *Kommando* Elbe had failed to deflect the Liberators and Fortresses from their objectives. The 'Mighty Eighth' had withstood every measure that the Luftwaffe had thrown against it – however radical – and had emerged as the undisputed victor in the daylight battle for the skies of the Reich.

By 1320 hrs it was all over. The surviving Messerschmitts of *Kommando* Elbe broke away and began heading back to base. But some 50-60 of its young pilots were never to return.

One victim of a ramming attack that made it back to base on 7 April 1945 was the 100th BG's B-17G 43-38514, which displays massive damage to its tailfin, rudder and port tailplane. The slashing wounds inflicted by the unknown Bf 109's propeller blades are clearly evident

APPENDICES

COLOUR PLATES

1

Fw 190A-6 'White 7' of Oberleutnant Ottmar Zehart,
Sturmstaffel **1, Dortmund, January 1944**
Most, if not all, of *Sturmstaffel* 1's original complement of
aircraft were given the same red Defence of the Reich aft
fuselage bands as worn by their host *Gruppe* at Dortmund,
Major Rudolf-Emil Schnoor's I./JG 1. Although not yet fitted
with armoured glass canopy protection, this particular
example does feature cockpit side armour. It was in 'White
7' that Oberleutnant Zehart reportedly claimed the *Staffel's*
first victory – a B-17 downed on 11 January 1944.

2

Fw 190A-6 'White 1' of Major Hans-Günter von Kornatzki,
Staffelkapitän Sturmstaffel **1, Dortmund, January 1944**
By mid-January 1944 *Sturmstaffel* 1's early A-6s had
undergone several changes. Note the wood-framed
armoured glass panels protecting the sides of the canopy in
line with the pilot's head (the so-called 'blinkers', or
'blinders'). More visually striking, however, is the unit's
adoption of distinctive black-white-black aft fuselage bands,
which were presumably to aid recognition in the air (and to
differentiate from I./JG 1's continuing use of red bands).
Although officially assigned as the *Staffelkapitän's* machine,
von Kornatzki apparently rarely flew this particular aircraft.

3

Fw 190A-6 'White 2' of Gefreiter Gerhard Vivroux,
Sturmstaffel **1, Dortmund, February 1944**
An obvious refinement to Vivroux's fully armoured
Sturmjäger is the large unit badge briefly sported by the
machines of *Sturmstaffel* 1 during the early weeks of 1944.
After claiming five B-17s with the *Staffel*, Gerhard Vivroux
subsequently served with IV.(*Sturm*)/JG 3. He died in
hospital on 25 October 1944 from wounds sustained 19
days earlier, having added a further five heavy bombers
and a single P-51 to his score.

4

Fw 190A-7 'White 8' of Feldwebel Werner Peinemann,
Sturmstaffel **1, Salzwedel, March 1944**
One of the *Staffel's* early A-7s, again fully armoured but
minus its fuselage-mounted MG 131 machine guns. Note
that the unit badge has already disappeared, but that the
hitherto plain spinner now wears a broad white spiral.
Previously a flying instructor, Werner Peinemann was
killed in a take-off accident at Welzow on 28 September
1944 when serving as a leutnant with II.(*Sturm*)/JG 4.

5

Fw 190A-7 'White 10' of *Sturmstaffel* **1, Salzwedel, March
1944**
There is little to distinguish this A-7 from Peinemann's

machine in Profile 4, other than the more tightly spiralled
spinner. This may be the 'White 10' put down on its belly
at Salzwedel on 8 April by Leutnant Siegfried Müller, who
was later appointed *Staffelkapitän* first of 16. and then
13.(*Sturm*)/JG 3, before ending the war with 17 victories
and flying the Me 262 jet with JG 7.

6

Fw 190A-7 'White 20' of Major Hans-Günter von Kornatzki,
Staffelkapitän Sturmstaffel **1, Salzwedel, March 1944**
The *Staffelkapitän's* preferred mount was this 'White 20'
(a choice of numeral perhaps influenced by the *Staffel's*
previous service alongside I./JG 1 at Dortmund, where the
Gruppenkommandeur's machine also wore a white '20' in
place of its earlier command chevron). Note the small
refinement to the aft fuselage bands, the black outer
bands now being thinly edged in white. It was in this
aircraft that Leutnant Gerhard Dost was shot down and
killed on 6 March shortly after claiming a Fortress for his
first victory.

7

Fw 190A-7 'White 14' of *Sturmstaffel* **1, Salzwedel,
April 1944**
Also wearing thinly edged aft fuselage bands, this rather
densely mottled A-7 – a late delivery – may well have been
one of the machines the unit had on strength when it was
incorporated into IV.(*Sturm*)/JG 3 'Udet' as that *Gruppe's*
new 11. *Staffel* on 8 May 1944.

8

Fw 190A-8/R2 'Yellow 17' of Unteroffizier Willi Unger,
12.(*Sturm*)/JG 3, Barth, May 1944
Among IV.(*Sturm*)/JG 3's first Fw 190s were the 12. *Staffel*
machines fitted with the rearward-firing, under-fuselage
rocket launcher tube. The weapon is clearly seen here,
together with JG 3's plain white Defence of the Reich band
(with truncated IV. *Gruppe* 'wavy bar' symbol as
previously worn by the unit's Bf 109s). Note too the black
cowling and stylised 'lightning flash' around the exhaust
and cooling louvres, as well as the trim in the *Staffel*
colour yellow. Unteroffizier Unger was obviously one of
those who quickly dispensed with the canopy 'blinkers',
putting visibility before protection!

9

Fw 190A-8/R2 'Black 8' of Unteroffizier Willi Maximowitz,
IV.(*Sturm*)/JG 3, Dreux, June 1944
Ex-*Sturmstaffel* 1 pilot Unteroffizier Maximowitz flew
this 11.(*Sturm*)/JG 3 *Sturmbock* (also minus its 'blinkers')
on fighter-bomber missions over the Normandy
beachheads. It wears a generally similar finish and
markings to the machine in Profile 8, but as 11. *Staffel's*

identifying colour was black, the trim shown here may have been of the pilot's own choosing. Note, however, the small 'Winged U' *Geschwader* badge on the cowling.

10

Fw 190A-8/R2 'Blue 13' of Major Walther Dahl, *Geschwaderkommodore* JG 300, Illesheim, July 1944
Something of a 'mystery ship', this machine clearly belongs to IV.(*Sturm*)/JG 3, as witness the white aft fuselage band with black 'wavy bar' superimposed. Pictures of Dahl posing in the cockpit of this aircraft were probably taken in the immediate aftermath of the Oschersleben battle as part of the intensive propaganda campaign which followed hard on the heels of the 'victory'. The colour of the individual numeral has long been accepted as blue, but there appears to be no solid evidence to corroborate this.

11

Fw 190A-8/R2 'Black Double Chevron' of Hauptmann Wilhelm Moritz, *Gruppenkommandeur* IV.(*Sturm*)/JG 3, Memmingen, July 1944
Hauptmann Moritz's own aircraft at the time of the Oschersleben action wore a textbook set of unit and command markings, the white band identifying JG 3, the 'wavy bar' indicating IV. *Gruppe* and the double chevron signifying the pilot's position as the *Kommandeur* of the unit. It also featured the black cowling and 'lightning flash'. While no doubt influenced by the distinctive 'eagle's head' motif sported earlier by JG 2 in the west, it is reported that IV.(*Sturm*)/JG 3's paintwork was applied at the suggestion of Hauptmann Moritz himself.

12

Fw 190A-8/R2 'Black Double Chevron' of Hauptmann Wilhelm Moritz, *Gruppenkommandeur* IV.(*Sturm*)/JG 3, Schongau, August 1944
Within the space of a month, however, the appearance of IV.(*Sturm*)/JG 3's *Sturmböcke* had undergone a dramatic change. Gone were the black noses and aft fuselage markings. The *Gruppe's* aircraft now displayed just the machine's individual number (or, as here, command symbol) on an otherwise plain factory finish of camouflage greys. Perhaps Hauptmann Moritz had had a change of mind, deciding that his unit should not advertise its presence in the air – and thus make itself a special target for US fighters – but rather blend in with the rest of the *Jagdgruppen* attacking the bomber streams.

13

Fw 190A-8/R2 'Black 3' of Obergefreiter Gerhard Kott, II.(*Sturm*)/JG 4, Welzow, August 1944
No such inhibitions for JG 4. When this *Jagdgeschwader* became part of the Defence of the Reich organisation, all of its machines, including the *Sturmböcke* of II. *Gruppe*, were given the same distinctive black-white-black aft fuselage identifying bands that had previously been worn by *Sturmstaffel* 1. Note also JG 4's plumed knight's helmet badge on the cowling. Gerhard Kott had come to 6.(*Sturm*)/JG 4 via IV.(*Sturm*)/JG 3. After serving as an instructor, he would return to his original unit in the closing days of the war.

14

Fw 190A-8/R2 'White 16' of Oberfähnrich Franz Schaar, 5.(*Sturm*)/JG 4, Welzow, September 1944
Very similar in finish to the machine in Profile 13, Schaar's *Fratz III* (see name below windscreen) shows that II.(*Sturm*)/JG 4's pilots also decided to dispense with their canopy 'blinkers' in very short order. As its name implies, this was Schaar's third 'White 16'. Having written-off the first two earlier in the month, a wounded Franz Schaar would belly-land *'Fratz III'* after claiming a B-24 on 27 September.

15

Fw 190A-8/R2 'White 7' of 7.(*Sturm*)/JG 300, Erfurt-Bindersleben, September 1944
Emulating IV.(*Sturm*)/JG 3's current anonymity (see Profile 12), II.(*Sturm*)/JG 300's early *Sturmböcke* flew in standard factory grey finish, with just the machine's individual number ahead of the fuselage cross and a horizontal II. *Gruppe* bar to the rear of it. Nothing here to tell any attacking US fighter pilot that he was lining up his sights on a *Sturm* aircraft – not even a tell-tale pair of 'blinkers'.

16

Fw 190A-8 'Yellow 12' of Unteroffizier Paul Lixfeld, 6.(*Sturm*)/JG 300, Erfurt-Bindersleben, September 1944
Another early II.(*Sturm*)/JG 300 machine, but very different from the near pristine 'White 7' in Profile 15, this battered specimen would appear to date back to the *Gruppe's* previous *'Wilde Sau'* days – as shown by the boar's head badge on the cowling. It had since been brought up to interim *Sturm* standard by the addition of armoured glass windscreen side panels and cockpit armour plating. Note the name *Muschi* on the latter, and the broad red aft fuselage band (JG 300's official Defence of the Reich recognition marking).

17

Fw 190A-8/R2 'Yellow 12' of Fahnenjunker-Oberfeldwebel Lothar Födisch, 6.(*Sturm*)/JG 300, Erfurt-Bindersleben, September 1944
A definitive II.(*Sturm*)/JG 300 *Sturmbock* of the period in terms of finish, markings and equipment (armoured glass windscreen side panels and cockpit armour plating, but no 'blinkers'). Lothar Födisch would be killed on 7 October in sister ship 'Yellow 15'. This particular machine (Wk-Nr. 681513) would go down over Silesia on 17 December when serving as 8. *Staffel's* 'Blue 15'.

18

Fw 190A-8/R2 'Yellow 1' of Feldwebel Ewald Preiss, 6.(*Sturm*)/JG 300, Löbnitz, October 1944
Another from the ranks of 6. *Staffel*, Ewald Preiss' 'Yellow 1' was presumably delivered to II.(*Sturm*)/JG 300 complete with 'blinkers' – note the row of rivet holes on the forward part of the sliding canopy frame where the armoured glass panel has been removed. This machine also bears a personal name – *Gloria* – below the cockpit just behind the panel of external armour.

19

Fw 190A-8/R2 'Red 1' of Leutnant Klaus Bretschneider, *Staffelkapitän* 5.(*Sturm*)/JG 300, Löbnitz, November 1944
First of a trio of well-known 5. *Staffel* aircraft operating out of Löbnitz late in 1944, the name on Klaus

Bretschneider's 'Red 1' says everything that needs to be said about its pilot – 'Rauhbautz' translates best as 'Tough guy', and if this is *Rauhbautz* number VII, then he must have got through at least six earlier machines! Wk-Nr. 682204 would be the last, however. Leutnant Bretschneider, winner of one of only eight Knight's Crosses awarded to *Sturm* pilots during the latter half of 1944, was flying the 'Red 1' depicted here when he was shot down by P-51s on 24 December.

20

Fw 190A-8 'Red 19' of Unteroffizier Ernst Schröder, 5.(*Sturm*)/JG 300, Löbnitz, November 1944

Unteroffizier Schröder's 'Red 19' – possibly the best known, and certainly the most frequently illustrated, of all II.(*Sturm*)/JG 300's *Sturm* aircraft – also ended its days after tangling with USAAF Mustangs, although Ernst Schröder himself did not help matters by inadvertently flying the damaged Fw 190 through the top of a large tree, as related in the accompanying text! The inscription *Kölle alaaf!* beneath the cockpit, the latter of which appears not to be fitted with external armour, is a local dialect expression often heard being shouted during Cologne's annual carnival. An approximate English equivalent would be 'Up with Cologne!'.

21

Fw 190A-8/R2 'Red 8' of Unteroffizier Matthäus Erhardt, 5.(*Sturm*)/JG 300, Löbnitz, November 1944

Last of the three 5. *Staffel* luminaries, Matthäus Erhardt regularly flew as *Katschmarek* (wingman) to *Staffelkapitän* Klaus Bretschneider. At just 19 years of age, Erhardt was one of the youngest pilots in the unit – a fact he cheerfully acknowledged by christening his machine *Pimpf* (Youngster). Erhardt's combat career came to an end during the last great air battle of 14 January 1945 when he was forced to bale out with a shattered knee. Like Ernst Schröder, he was credited with a final score of seven confirmed victories.

22

Fw 190A-8/R2 'Red 10' of Feldwebel Karl-Heinz Rusack, 5.(*Sturm*)/JG 300, Löbnitz, December 1944

A fourth member of 5. *Staffel*, Feldwebel Rusack's 'Red 10' bears very little resemblance to the three machines illustrated in the three previous profiles. It has an unusually heavy dapple camouflage finish overall and carries no aft fuselage Defence of the Reich band. Karl-Heinz Rusack was wounded just 11 days before the war's end.

23

Fw 190A-8/R2 'Black 3' of 14.(*Sturm*)/JG 3, Gütersloh, December 1944

Another even more nondescript *Sturmbock* of IV.(*Sturm*)/JG 3 during its closing battles on the western front during the winter of 1944-45. When dispensing with its white Defence of the Reich bands, it appears that the IV. *Gruppe* 'wavy bar' symbol was also dropped. Perhaps it was felt that as the only *Gruppe* within the *Geschwader* flying Fw 190s, no additional means of identification was necessary. This particular machine may have been the 'Black 3' in which Feldwebel Josef Sommer was shot down over Belgium on 24 December.

24

Fw 190A-8/R2 'White 11' of Gefreiter Walter Wagner, 5.(*Sturm*)/JG 4, Babenhausen, December 1944

If Ernst Schröder's *Kölle alaaf!* is today the most illustrated machine of II.(*Sturm*)/JG 300, then Gefreiter Wagner's 'White 11' must, without doubt, have been the most photographed *Sturmbock* of II.(*Sturm*)/JG 4. It can hardly have been otherwise, for Wagner belly-landed   Wk-Nr. 681497 at St Trond, home of the Thunderbolts of the US Ninth Air Force's 48th and 404th FGs, at the height of Operation *Bodenplatte* on New Year's Day 1945. The 404th apparently got to 'White 11' first . . .

25

Fw 190A-8/R2 '00-L' of the 404th FG, Ninth Air Force, St Trond, January 1945

. . . and this is what they did to it! Getting the *Sturmbock* back onto its feet, they gave it a completely new paint job – bright red overall, but with JG 4's unit badge carefully left untouched on the cowling. It has been suggested that the 'squadron markings' on the fuselage were meant to be read as 'Oh, oh – 'ell'. The 'serial' on the tailfin (the date of the *Bodenplatte* attack) is self-explanatory. Although a replacement BMW engine was found and fitted, 'White 11' was reportedly never flown under its new management, and the 404th had regretfully to leave its prize behind when the group moved on to Kelz, in Germany.

26

Fw 190A-8/R2 'White 6' of Leutnant Gustav Salffner, *Staffelkapitän* 7.(*Sturm*)/JG 300, Löbnitz, January 1945

After apparently dispensing with its red tail bands for a short period during the winter of 1944-45 (see Profile 22), II.(*Sturm*)/JG 300 was ordered to re-apply bands of a different colour – blue-white-blue – early in the new year. 'Gustl' Salffner's 'White 6' not only shows these new markings to advantage (with a white horizontal II. *Gruppe* bar superimposed), but also displays what is reported to be the Salffner family crest on (both sides of) the engine cowling.

27

Fw 190A-8 'Black 2' of 14.(*Sturm*)/JG 3, Prenzlau, February 1945

In contrast to II.(*Sturm*)/JG 300's colourful new Defence of the Reich bands, the machines of IV.(*Sturm*)/JG 3 retained their anonymity after being transferred to the eastern front early in 1945. This fairly clean looking example – there was no shortage of new aircraft, even at this late stage of the war – carries a 250kg bomb for low-level *Jabo* operations against Red Army units along the line of the River Oder.

28

Fw 190A-8 'White 15' of Oberleutnant Anatol Rebane, II.(*Sturm*)/JG 4, Glücksburg, April 1945

II.(*Sturm*)/JG 4 also deleted their distinctive, and highly visible, black-white-black aft fuselage bands when transferred to the eastern front. The area behind 'White 15's' horizontal *Gruppe* bar shows clear signs of overpainting. Note too the bulged canopy on this late-production A-8. Anatol Rebane was the second of two II.(*Sturm*)/JG 4 pilots, both Estonian volunteers, to fly to neutral Sweden shortly before the war's end in order to escape possible Soviet captivity.

SELECTED BIBLIOGRAPHY

ALSDORF, DIETRICH, *Rammjäger: Auf den Spuren des 'Elbe-Kommandos'.* Podzun-Pallas, Wölfersheim, 2001

BETHKE, HERBERT and HENNIG, FRIEDHELM, *Jagdgeschwader 300 ('Wilde Sau').* Private publication (two volumes)

FREEMAN, ROGER A, *Mighty Eighth War Diary.* Jane's, London, 1981

GIRBIG, WERNER, *im Anflug auf die Reichshauptstadt.* Motorbuch Verlag, Stuttgart, 1970

GIRBIG, WERNER, *Start im Morgengrauen.* Motorbuch Verlag, Stuttgart, 1973

GIRBIG, WERNER, *... mit Kurs auf Leuna.* Motorbuch Verlag, Stuttgart, 1980

GÜTH, FRANK, PAUL, AXEL and SCHUH, HORST, *Vom Feindflug nicht zurückgekehrt.* Helios, Aachen, 2001

HAMMEL, ERIC, *Air War Europa: Chronology 1942-1945.* Pacifica Press, California, 1994

HELD, WERNER, *Reichsverteidigung, die deutsche Tagjagd 1943-1945.* Podzun-Pallas, Friedberg 1988

HERRMANN, HAJO, *Bewegtes Leben, Kampf- und Jagdflieger 1935-1945.* Motorbuch Verlag, Stuttgart, 1984

MANRHO, JOHN and PÜTZ, RON, *Bodenplatte, the Luftwaffe's Last Hope.* Hikoki Publications, Crowborough, 2004

MOMBEEK, ERIC, *Sturmjäger, zur Geschichte des Jagdgeschwaders 4 und der Sturmstaffel 1 (two volumes).*

A.S.B.L. La Porte d'Hoves, Linkebeek, 1997 and 2000

MOMBEEK, ERIC, *Sturmstaffel 1 – Reich Defence 1943-44 The War Diary.* Classic Publications, Crowborough, 1999

OBERMAIER, ERNST, *Die Ritterkreuzträger der Luftwaffe 1939-1945, Band I: Jagdflieger.* Verlag Dieter Hoffmann, Mainz, 1966

PARKER, DANNY S, *To Win the Winter Sky – Air War over the Ardennes, 1944-1945.* Greenhill Books, London, 1994

PRICE, ALFRED, *Focke-Wulf Fw 190 at War.* Ian Allan Ltd, Shepperton, 1977

PRIEN, JOCHEN, *IV./Jagdgeschwader 3, Chronik des Einsatzes einer Jagdgruppe, 1943-1945.* Struve-Druck, Eutin, 1996

RODEIKE, PETER, *Focke-Wulf Jagdflugzeug Fw 190A, Fw 190D 'Dora', Ta 152H.* Struve-Druck, Eutin, 1998

ROSE, ARNO, *Radikaler Luftkampf, die Geschichte deutscher Rammjäger.* Motorbuch Verlag, Stuttgart, 1977

RUST, KENN C, *The 9th Air Force in World War II.* Aero Publishers Inc., Fallbrook, 1967

RUST, KENN C, *Fifteenth Air Force Story.* Historical Aviation Album, Temple City, 1976

SAFT, ULRICH, *Das bittere Ende der Luftwaffe.* Verlag-Saft, Langenhagen, 1992

WEIR, ADRIAN, *The Last Flight of the Luftwaffe, The Fate of Schulungslehrgang Elbe, 7 April 1945.* Arms and Armour, London, 1997

INDEX

References to illustrations are shown in **bold**.
Colour Plate illustrations are prefixed 'cp.', with page and caption locators in brackets.